KITH

Illustrations by Karin Aue
Cover design by Jay Millar/Book*hug
Book design by Rebecca Wolff
Copyediting by Joshua Lam

John Singleton Copley, *Watson and the Shark*. 1778.
Used by permission of National Gallery of Art. Washington, DC,
with grateful acknowledgment of Sputnik & Fizzle.

Published in the United States by Fence Books
110 Union Street
Second Floor
Hudson NY 12534

Published in Canada by Book*hug

www.fenceportal.org

This book was printed by Versa Press and distributed by Small
Press Distribution and Consortium Book Sales and Distribution.

Library of Congress Cataloguing in Publication Data
Victor, Divya [1983–]
Kith/Divya Victor

Library of Congress Control Number: 2017951098

ISBN 13: 978-1-9342005-7-5

First Edition
10 9 8 7 6 5 4 3 2

DIVYA VICTOR

KITH

Fence Books (Albany) & BookThug (Toronto)

Prologue

You were between terminals. You saw a woman— her eyes
darting between the Departures board and the crumpled
printout in her hand. You walked her to her gate, which was in
the opposite direction from yours. You learned, as we do, of her
occupation her hometown her mother's health and you learned
something of what she was paid for washing dishes mopping
floors changing the nappies chopping vegetables for a family
of five that was not hers to love or live for. You felt the heat of
her skin and recognized the bag she was carrying— borrowed
from her employer who had received it as a freebie for some
expensive eye cream or cologne. Your own wife or sister or
mother or daughter might have this bag stuffed in a closet filled
with clothes that became too small or too wrong for the season
or occasion or audience. And in this bag you saw that she had
squirreled away four cans of Coke through Security— one given
to her for every three months of good and honest service by her
foreign employers. She was carrying them home for her children
because they had never tasted it. She had plans to buy ice to
buy a small plot of land to save money for the bricks to sell her
gold for cement. She was departing for Colombo and you for
Chennai. When you left her at the gate, she pulled a warm and
heavy can of Coke from her bag and offered it to you.

And when you told us this story and when you began to explain
how her offering had made you feel, your trembling hands—
because of habit and manner— reached towards your eyes and
hid from us their misery. And when you did this, in all of us a
wave of warm blood convulsed and pooled together to catch
your tears and to carry her to safety in our stories.

For those they described as the "naked niggers [of India], members of a race . . . all such miserable, fawning, cringing, slavish cowards, especially when flogged for they don't resist but shriek frightfully for mercy."

& for those who made song from the shriek frightful

I am not distrustful of my nostalgia—I think nostalgia can be a weapon in a cultural milieu where you are expected to feel only shame for what you have left behind—but I do want to ask what it means to remember.

AMITAVA KUMAR, *Bombay—London—New York*

Ultimately, it is this fraternity that makes it possible ... for so many millions of people, not so much to kill, as willingly to die for such limited imaginings.

BENEDICT ANDERSON, *Imagined Communities*

From another epic another history. From the missing narrative. From the multitude of narratives. Missing. From the chronicles. For another telling for other recitations.

THERESA HAK KYUNG CHA, *Dictee*

Loss has made a tenuous we.

RACHEL ZOLF, *Neighbour Procedure*

neither your mother nor your father nor your sister nor your
brother; neither your grandmother nor your grandfather nor your
aunt by blood nor your uncle by blood; neither your child nor your
grandchild nor your great grandparent nor your great grandchild;
neither of this generation nor the next nor the one prior; neither
your cousin by blood nor your cousin by bone; neither inheriting
nose nor skin nor brow nor boat; neither bestowing flesh nor tooth
nor hair nor gait; neither in a manner of laughing nor holding a
plate; neither descended from nor ascending to; neither named
for nor named after; neither of brood nor blood nor stock nor
pool; neither possessing by claim nor disowned by name; neither
baptized at the ancestral font nor buried in the shared grave;
neither living nor dead nor born nor bred; neither passed on nor
passing away; neither like nor unlike nor resembling tissue and
cartilage; neither by birthright nor by death rites nor by divination
nor miracle; neither by gene nor gestation; neither by womb nor
tomb nor cuckold nor platoon *b u t* by what is sensed or seen or
heard or felt in what moves between those not of blood and yet
belonging together either on land or in air or in water or on paper;
either through name or race or face or place of birth or blame;
either as sign or shibboleth or overheard epithet; either as mark
on a forehead or caught in crosshairs; either for paycheck or
paper or map or license or visa; either by the queue or queue or
queen or quill; either by mandate or state or decree or fiat of fate;
either in law or labor or abode or abhorred; either by hell or high
water; either by tongue or trade or tendency to wander; either as
a manner of walking into rooms or crossing the arms; either by
headdress or footwear or part of hair; either by grain or meat or
milk or holy book; as the days of the week or the names for the
moon; as a manner of love or as a manner of hate; as a manner of
leaning or standing erect; either by ritual or by roads taken; by the
way something pleats or drapes or hangs or is latent; as a way you
move or are at rest by passing or failing another's test; either as a
way of knowing or being known; either by the way a "we" exists
or does not when we are not home; either as targets or by treason;
either as a question of resemblance or in answer to a name: *kith.*

DROMOMANIE

By the term ambulatory automatism [*dromomanie*] is understood a
pathological syndrome appearing in the form of intermittent attacks
during which the patient, carried away by an irresistible impulse,
leaves his home and makes an excursion or journey justified by
no reasonable motive. The attack ended, the subject unexpectedly
finds himself on an unknown road or in a strange town. Swearing
by all the gods never again to quit his penates, he returns home but
sooner or later a new attack provokes a new escapade.

ALBERT PITRES, *Leçons cliniques sur l'hystérie et
l'hypnotisme: faites à l'hôpital Saint-André de Bordeaux* (1891)

in one such case a woman was found so forcefully fornicating
with her feet the soil under her that they thought she was
attempting to bury her own body while standing upright. when
pressed, she confessed that she had heard of travel and was
attempting to push her body through to the other side of the
world

— *there are many such cases*

in one such case a man so beaten by debt two wives and four girl
children menstruating in orchestrated vengeance against the greasy
rupees in his pocket rolled his bedding and straw mat and carried
them out of his hut after he'd shat out his gruel and before the
cock crowed into the cadmium sky

— *later this story was told to four girls,*
all wives, pulling straw matting and
feathers from their cunts smelling of
sleep and gruel— *the afterbirth stamped*
and dated

in one such case a man was promised a wall made of gold bricks
in a land where palm trees bled almond milk and oases of honey
pooled wherever one stood and so he took his passport out of
the rinsed milk-bag and offered it to an agent who flew him to a
desert and left him there where he drank his own piss and never
returned until his wife gone bone dry in waiting married a man
with an identical mustache years later

— later this story was told by the
neighbor of a policeman greased with
Palmolive margarine and lifting a
grinding stone above his head and
onto a sleeping infant

in one such case a woman embroidering the name of her fourth
child into the mantelpiece tapestry was called by her husband to
suckle oil from the Persian gulf in a city that clotted around an
oasis where centuries ago star crossed lovers failed each other—
Layla and Majnun: she dying in waiting, he walking miles and
kissing every wall to know if she lived behind it— and from which
she would return without her hair and with a spool of black
thread to spell again

*— later this story was told to children
in a kitchen while smoothing the ruffled
mackerel gills and sharpening knives
on grey slabs of granite drawn from a
quarry where men had fallen over and
over in love with their own destinies*

in one such case a man who wore a snake around his neck used
a mountain as a churning rod and a serpent as a churning rope
and curdled an ocean of milk until the mountain sank so far into
the cream that he swam in his skirts and turned himself into a
turtle to carry the mountain on his back miles under milk fat

— later this story was told to two girls
unbraiding hair slick with coconut oil
and tied with polyester ribbons: the
stuff of couch stuffing yacht insulation
holograms bank notes

in one such case a woman exchanging aluminum paise for whole
mackerel was called by her father through the gardener who was
sent by the scullery maid who had heard from the family's jeweler
that the bloom of gold which secured the daughter's marriage to
the man from the land of arrows had a heart of wax and so this
woman walked backward oily pomfret scales flashing at her gold
bangles and pink roe spilling to the earth until she reached the
land of arrows and rent each shaft in two and returned wearing
fletching in her hair like firecracker flowers— genus *crossandra*;
lifecycle *perennial*

— *and later there was no later*

in one such case a man searching for his wife who had been held captive by a demon with ten heads and with a sword that sliced the wings of vultures built a bridge across the ocean and when he returned with her flung over his shoulder he asked that she sit in a wooden pyre on fire where she burned and burned while the three-striped palm squirrels stroked by her husband on his quest to find her flourished on fallen gooseberries and cashews

> — later this story was told to a
> classroom staring at a blackboard
> gone white with chalk guarded by
> one sentry spitting beetlenut into
> a copper spittoon and the other
> scratching an ashy elbow

in one such case a man who had been driven off a cliff by a soldier with frayed epaulettes pulled from the linings of his pockets anti-tank missiles and anvils and muzzleloader rifles like feathers off a batshit bantam and when he faced the salty rock he finally pulled out his compass and sunk it to sea his feet fast behind him sooty feathered and on fire

— later this story was told to a girlchild squatting on freshly washed ground her ass powdered her skirts ironed her two feet planted and floating like any other rhizome ready to be braised sliced and served at a wedding

— later this story was told to a child by a child
traveling away from herself

NO MAN'S LAND

a migrant is a disputed
territory over which there
is *our* a disagreement
this is an *my* attempt
at resemblance *my*
a body reaching a *mine*
an agreement with his

FIRST ATTEMPT: TO SPREAD MYSELF THIN
OVER NO MAN'S LAND

I take a small rolling pin the size of a sausage which is ground meat
with a skin around it | I take a rolling pin made of maple shorn of
bark and tapered by a steel rasp sharpened on a stone which is to
say a maple shrub a mature riparian split in rings and shedding
its lobed and palmate leaves shaking in the truck on its way its
racemes and umbels jangling in its chest to the orchestral rumble
of the I-405 this *acer glabrum* roaring towards becoming a rolling
pin the size of a sausage small enough for a child's hand to take
and hold | I take this rolling pin and hold back my left earlobe
with my right hand but having no third hand with which to both
lift my earlobe and roll over my lobe with this small rolling pin |
I lay myself on this floor made of strips of splintered pine so thin
like a million chopsticks and hope that my weight will pin me to
these pine boards the heft of my head is pressing my lobe to the
floor and I am dreaming of a paperweight big enough and made
of glass as if the silica mined from the gaping pits of dunes and
dredged from the ocean bed the powdery remains of the sweat of
beaches in this glass paper weight will be heavy enough | I hope I
will be heavy enough to press down on my earlobe long enough to
let me lift this small rolling pin in both my hands and as I look up
at the ceiling that has been over me this whole time I press and roll
over my earlobe with this small rolling pin in an attempt to spread
myself thin over no man's land when I am ten years old and falling
asleep on my mother's lap and her left hand is crusted in a shell
of chappati dough which she has left to dry rather than wake me
while my father reads *The Hindu* where in full color a fleet of F-15s
is parked at the Al Kharj Naval Base and the fuzz of pixels is a
peach skin unrolled over the desert storm and folded in half before
lunch

SECOND ATTTEMPT: TO COLLECT ALL MY MOLES
TO MAKE A MOLEHILL ON NO MAN'S LAND

I take a letter opener left to my mother by my grandfather who
received it from his father who drove into a tree travelling in
a motorcar a flask quaking in his vest and when the priest's
vestments quivered at the funeral asking for the fees yet to be
paid before the choir would Ave the grand lad | I take this letter
opener made of a sliver of elephant ivory drawn from the tusks of
a wrinkled grey corpse just so many finger clippings when seen
from above a thousand creamy crescent moons fallen on the dust
| I take this letter opener and slip its tip under the corner of my
eye where my first mole sits like a grain of dark gram or a long
lentil sheltered by lashes and behind glasses | I take that letter
opener to snap it up from my skin like a red waxen seal pressed
on my eye as viscous black bitumen or the pus-beige of beeswax
colored with vermilion doused in shellac bathed in turpentine and
pressed onto the corner of my eye with a signet ring worn on the
wrinkled knuckles of some so-and-so and so I slip the ivory sliver
under the mole to split it from my skin and open this envelope
| I want this as the first mole for my collection but the wax has
been set on fire and left to harden sealing my skin at the first
place where I can flap it open the correspondence flittering out
pages and pages in an attempt to collect my first mole to make a
molehill on no man's land when I am eleven years old and falling
asleep on my mother's lap and her left hand is holding a sheaf of
postcards from Benghazi where my father churns salt water from
the Mediterranean sea into sweet water slumbering in a holy font
nestled in the portico between the six Doric columns of the Old
Cathedral wearing and tearing its marbled skin off

THIRD ATTEMPT: TO MAKE CONTOUR LINES
OF MY STRETCH MARKS TO DENOTE TERRAIN
ON NO MAN'S LAND

I take a rubber glove from the toilet bucket which has in it a
scrubbing brush and a plunger and a mate for the rubber glove
which is pink like flesh under the foreskin but worn in patches
from rubbing against cement the volcanic ash and pulverized brick
pasted over concrete pockmarked grey | I take this rubber glove and
try to get a grip on the slippery waves of white where the creases of
my armpits announce my arms where the hitch of my hip relents
to peel where the yarn of the stretch marks a cirrus which moves
swift over the rump and striates where the skin pinches itself and
blanches from expansions and contractions the wearing and tearing
of itself | I hope this glove grips the stretch mark long enough to
lift and tug and unravel a skein of scars to lift the strings of stretch
marks and lay them down on no man's land to make contour lines
on this curve which has endured nothing but territory so I tug and
strip the white and whittled marks of my body's gloat swelling the
years of nothing but growth and they cling so tight so I lift this
glove and exhale so my skin sacks off and puddles at the joints
where wrists were where ankles accumulate in folds where they are
handcuffed and bootlaced | I exhale but the yarn wraps tighter this
brown paper package tied up with string my favorite things wrapped
tighter and tighter and strung by the stretch marks that sluice from
the small hairs blond on brown rump linguine limp and ripping
the hairs trapped in the yarn of these marks dermichronologous
the early wood spring wood and late wood of my spine and what
of me hardens when I take the rubber glove | I want to pick up
the lattice of stretch marks and lay them down on no man's land

bottomed out from my bottom like lean or slope *isopleth isarithm isoline* a series of stenciled varves endlessly with no interior where I never was a verse of lines on no man's land but only growing to become this body when I am twelve years old and falling asleep on my mother's lap and her left hand is holding a limp pair of blue chiffon stockings pulled from a *par avion* envelope sent from the fruit market in Tripoli where my father sells his leather jacket bought second hand in the Trichy black market in exchange for flannels chocolate and double-helix gold chokers for mother and daughter one two inches shorter the other two inches longer to wrap their necks to their shoulders

KITH

White America is still poisoned by racism, which is as native
to our soil as pine trees, sagebrush, and buffalo grass.
MARTIN LUTHER KING JR.
"Testament of Hope," *Playboy* (1969)

ர	l̲	as in *red*
ள	ḷ	as in *look*
ற	r̲	as in *room*
ண	n̲	as in *night*
ஸ	ś	as in *sow*
ஜ	j	as in *joke*

Red Maple	*acer rubrum*	red as in *blood*
Lead Plant	*amorpha canescens*	dark purple as in *bruise*
Redbud	*cercis canadensis*	deep pink as in *lesion*
Nodding Marigold	*bidens cernua*	yellow as in *pus*
Shellbark Hickory	*carya laciniosa*	green as in *fester*
Joe-Pye Weed	*eupatorium maculatum*	mauve as in *graze*

And how many countries are there in the world?
Two.
Two?
India and Forin.
And where do you live?
In that one.

AGE 6

FORIGN

FORRIEN

FURAYN

FIRANG

PHUREIGN

PHURAYN

FAWRUN

FORESWEAR

SOVEREIGN

FORBEAR

FORIENG

FAWNING

FÍRINNE

OR AREN'T

ORION

ORIGIN

FORIGIN

FORAGE

RAGE HERE

FORAGE HERE

PAPER PEOPLE

what I know is this
when my grandmother
       dies it will be in a place
where she knew no one but us
what I do is this
write: when my grandmother
       dies it will be in a place
where we knew
no one but her

where were you when it will happen
the earth above us
the moon below
the crow caw an atlas
of mangle

தென்பாண்டி சீமையிலே
தேரோடும் வதியிலே
மான் போல வந்தவனே
யார் அடித்தாரோ
யார் அடித்தாரோ
வளரும் பிறையே தேயாதே
இனியும் அழுது தேம்பாதே
அழுதா மனசு தாங்காதே

In the town of Thenpandi
On the streets where chariots race
You who stole in like a brown fawn: who beat you down?
Who beat you down? Who beat you down?

O, dear waxing moon—do not wane
Do not, even now, weep out your pain
If you wail, my heart won't bear it
When you wail, my heart can't bear it

PULAMAIPITHAN & MAESTRO ILAYARAAJA, *Nayagan*

HOW TO SURVIVE ON LAND IF YOU ARE MADE OF PAPER

keep variations
on an exit handy
mend the sandals & eat enough
dirt to grow
accustomed to waiting
on new ground

walk up to strangers
with maps & beg
an interpretation & ask
them to divine your path
past the Walmart & into
the parking lot where you live
in a Toyota hatching
suitcases unpacking
plans

make of your walk a wall
make of your arms an armory
make of a memory nothing but selfsame
but in the darkness of movie theatres
memorize the faces with lined eyes
unlined foreheads untied
frenulums undone
sternums; walk home with
the dead flittering out
of your thrifted coats
cinematic litter— did you see have you seen
us do
like this

line the cupboards
with old visas; rim the stamps
with tea cups & wait
for them to be upset
by guests hold
your breath

stuff the walls with hair
shorn for devotions
save the coupons for coffins
elsewhere

press no hibiscus into old books
undo your face every night with metal
& mercury; drag your mothers
out from the roots of your hair
with bleach & heat

nail your feet to the rails
& suck the words
from mouths like fillings clinking into basins

from them
smelt
the metal
& make eyes for your dead

learn to stay
wary of waves; weave
teeth into grins; stand
in line; disappear
in plain sight; hide
a language like a wetness
for the wrong one

draw chalk lines between
your children & ask them to call
each other what you called
your sister your brother & gather
back the parts
of their name every time
every time they toss them
on the streets throw them in the trash

clean them
letter for letter
in the cold tub

say yes please thank you often & with nodding
never shake the head to mean yes or no; never mean anything other

count the old knees & buy the ointments in bulk to stave off a
winter; tell the old knees the stories of their kneeling, the stories
of their standing hard against the gallop of gunfire, the wallop of
leather

build altars from crates & unframe
all the photographs reframe
them in another apartment
        with the newspaper windows the cardboard
        furniture the boardwalk hot fat waft
in dollar store frames that grow soggy during the winter
        that distend the faces
        & turn the eyes into oyster flesh

replace strings with buttons; replace
trains with cars; replace
food with fend

clear spaces
on beds; rinse
the disposable forks
fall awake
to borrowed weather

close the doors
twice as often as you open them
refuse the mailman his greeting; rush at letters
& make from the envelopes a small iron lung

spin sugar from peaching light; consider
your neighbor
the other neighbor's neighbor

paint fences with blood; write
of the dark ones on the white
palms of small things
with henna & glance at harvest moons
hold a sieve up to view
a husband's face meshed
in DMV queues consulate queues
say *you say you say we*
count the pieces
of luggage; count
the reincarnations at Costco

practice walks down the aisle off the plank; borrow pans

save Coke bottles and fill them
with frying grease watching
for gnats; iron curtains
with burning books

your walls wear two clocks
tell two times; love both
enough to forget the difference
when you call home, where the arms point

park the car
like an unhinged gate

borrow small sums
sorrow your savings
into the children's acronyms
M.A., J.D., M.B.B.S., Ph.D., D.D.S.,
M.B.A., N.R.I., U.S.A.

in dreams make ash from dung; draw
drawls from wells and bury fires in glass jars
to remember your mother's mother
who has forgotten her mother's mother's mother's
child's child's child; fold her sari in twos fours eights
keep pace of that face
down the line
account for her too because
she won't *herself thereself theirself*
how to say
your eyes are like no one

arrange the children
in the closet; make of their skin
a resemblance to papers
live off the fat of the landmine

wipe the pews
when your knees smear
their grain; leave no trace
dog-ear no holy book
admit nothing
of the drone; bless yourself
& pray for the sick who make others
sick; understand dispossession to mean
we too once possessed
were so too
by someone

pull from your own elbows the twine to bind & hog-tie
your self to a passerby; sing
your new national anthem into their ear

mourn your dead in letters
bury your dead in the sky

செல்லமே   let the eagles eat their hearts out
let the eagles eat their hearts out

PAPER BOATS

I fly like paper, get high like planes
If you catch me at the border I got visas in my name

MATHANGI ARULPRAGASAM

catamaran |ˌkatəməˈran|
noun

a yacht or other boat with twin hul கட்டுமரம்

ORIGIN early 17th cent.: from Tamil
kaṭṭumaram, literally "*tied wood*"

Go to a place with no water
& drink

Go to a place with no trees
& find shade

Go to a place with no bodies
& find yours buried there

00A.

This is the front of your body

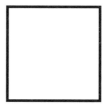

You may use any kind of body to fold into this boat, this catamaran

I am using a typical body with a slightly different color for front and back of the boat

I am using anything I can find around the house that looks like my body or yours   ·

00B.

This is the back of your body

Start with the back of your body facing up

Fold the arms towards the chest along the axis of your spine

Draw tight the skin and press down using your thumbs to make creases on your skin

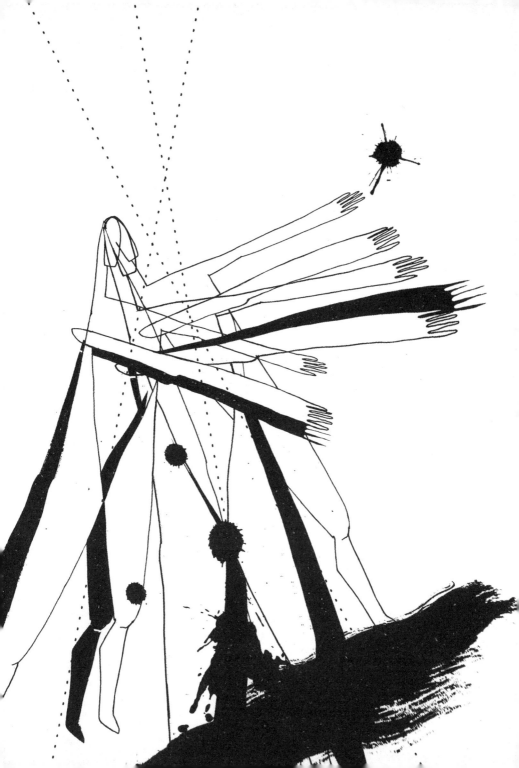

001.

This is your body facing backward; this is your face placed on the ground

002.

Fold yourself in half taking care to keep your spine from curving under the strain of the turn

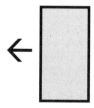

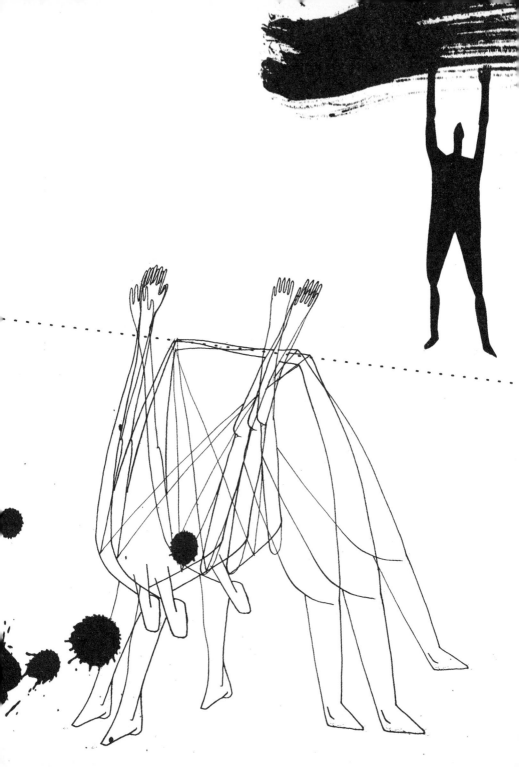

003.

Now unfold and press back your body to the ground, or flat against a wall or car

Ask another body to press against you to achieve the necessary flatness before moving on, before proceeding to fold again

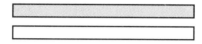

Now strip from your body everything that will stop it from lying absolutely flat

004.

Crease your body across your chest, creating an axis from your right palm to your left foot

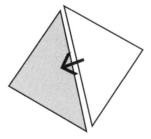

Touch your palm to your foot and hold your breath as your thumb presses down on any skin bubbling at the corners

Face the ground until your hands have pressed you flat, taking care to ensure that no extraneous skin or flesh leaves the edges or exceeds the boundaries of the boat you are making

00_.

Build a boat with twin hulls

One hull pointed East
One hull pointed West

Now build a body
that can sail this boat

Now find the wind
that can carry us home

00_.

Now find the wind
that can carry us home

WATER

Once they found a man made of distance— a coat of shells, a wig of weeds— and at his breast a suckling book made of salty skin, stamped on its chubble joints, its fatty folds— us, us— visas. Two webbed palms cupping the downy document. *Motherless child,* they said, *let us buy you.*

Once it saw the man— *Was he waving or drowning?* It matters not: what is of the water returns to water— Once it saw the man, the boat rowed itself from the shore, folding fins out like a manta ray breaching into red spray, cartilage and cartridge inked out, flared into an X: marking this location and the boat's movement.

& then?

Once the man was finally harpooned and lanced to death, the boat towed him ashore, and, with small cranes sprouting from its fins, flensed his fat and boiled his bones clean to build a child up from flank to fo'c'sle; skull to stem; fore and aft.

& aft? What was aft?

That thing at the end, Child, this was everything that came after the boats came.

Aft was everything we became.

Child\ he said\ put out to deep water

and so we did

Child\ he said\ let down your net

and so we did

Child\ he said\ catch your fish

and so we waited

& they caught so many fish that their nets began to break

& so they cried to the others in other boats to come and help them

& so those others, they came to these others

& so they, together, filled both boats so full that they began to sink

& so the boats began to sink with fish

WATER, WATER, EVERY WHERE,
NOR ANY DROP TO DRINK.

Pearl Oysters

The soft tissue of a living oyster produces a pearl to protect itself against foreign substances. The things that don't belong inside it become jewels to be strung up and hung. On some so-and-so's neck. A womb so supple and so alien: a mother of pearl and a mother at peril.

Pearl & Peril

At a McDonald's in the Fukushima prefecture
a child was injured by a piece of hard plastic
which was in her hot-fudge ice-cream sundae

At a McDonald's in the Aomori prefecture
a customer found a piece of blue vinyl
lodged in the white meat of her chicken nugget

At a McDonald's in the Osaka prefecture
a customer found a human tooth
chattering in her French fries

At a seafood restaurant in Tennessee
a woman biting into a fried oyster
pulled pearl after pearl from her mouth
fifty wet with grease and spit

Marine Snow

The bodies of dead animals pursued and eaten by predators sink slowly down to the sea floor. Life at the bottom is sustained by sinking flesh called marine snow. The *ampyroteuthis infernalis*, the "vampire squid from Hell" (neither vampire nor squid nor from Hell), pulses six hundred meters down in the lush ocean, demersal and blood flushed, wearing its own mouth around its neck like a velvet cape. Every day, it basks in marine snow; every day it eats the ocean. And at bottom, all depth is a kind of Hell.

Squid Beak

In the ocean, a rostrum is the cupped sharpness of the dorsal and lower mandibles of a squid's piercing mouthpart. On a naval ship, a rostrum is a beak-like extension of bronze and iron designed to wreck the hull of an enemy ship. In a public forum, a rostrum is the pulpit that hides your body and lets you open your mouth to the world. From which one will you speak— and in which one will you die— and for whom?

Ambergris

After a sperm whale sucks in a squid, it will vomit out its beak.
If it does not, the beak will travel through three hundred meters
of its digestive labyrinth. The crushing churn of the whale's four
stomachs can grind the squid's funnels and collars, its eight
arms, its three beating hearts. But it can't break a squid beak.
The whale's hind stomach hoards thousands of squid beaks
like a clacking library of bonemouths. To protect itself from
the scrape and drag of the squid beaks, the whale's intestines
produce a waxy ambergris— grey, fatty, flammable— a carrier
for a scent worn on your pulse.

Salted Fish

Look into its eyes; flip through its gills; scale it; cut off the head
at the gills and place it aside; flip it so its belly faces you; open
its belly from its anal fin to its gills; using your finger draw out
the guts; find the egg sack and place it aside; flank the fish open;
flense it; flatten it; fillet it and place it on the earth. Cover it with
salt. Leave it be. Leave it be. Call it அம்மா and wait for it to
answer.

Coup D'Etat

In France, this "blow against the state" refers to one thing.
Among indigenous North Americans a *coup* refers to the act of
touching an enemy or grazing an object belonging to an enemy
in order to claim it. And to claim him. You should imagine now
a very small, chicken-necked girl with flat, soft knees wobbling
on a black rock cupping the Indian Ocean in her hands— a
blow of foam to part the states along the line of fate. When they
read the palm of a girlchild, they read the fate line on the left
palm— the illiterate hand, the hand used to wipe the ass clean
of lunch.

Fathom

At one time, this meant "to embrace with arms wide open." At another time, this became a unit of measurement— a length of six feet. At yet another time, this came to mean "understanding" or "measurability," or its inverse: unfathomable depths were meanings that could not be reached by using one's own body as a unit of measurement. You should imagine now a woman with arms wide open diving into the Pacific Ocean, measuring it with her own body— unfathomable phantom— she a pantoum, a pun.

A B C D
B E D F
E G F H
G I (or A or C) H J (or A or C)

this is how an ocean is told

what is done with wet
& when
an inheritance—

Four interwoven quatrains
Three generations damp
Two oceans of wet
One boat

BLOOD

1. No English. Indian. Walking.

I'm writing about your article during July about the abuse
of Indian People. Well I'm here to state the other side. I hate
them, if you had to live near them you would also. We are an
organization called the Dotbusters. We have been around for 2
years. We will go to any extreme to get Indians to move out of
Jersey City. If I'm walking down the street and I see a Hindu and
the setting is right, I will hit him or her. We plan some of our
most extreme attacks such as breaking windows, breaking car
windows, and crashing family parties. We use the phone books
and look up the name Patel. Have you seen how many of them
there are? Do you even live in Jersey City? Do you walk down
Central Avenue and experience what it's like to be near them: we
have and we just don't want it anymore. You said that they will
have to start protecting themselves because the police cannot
always be there. They will never do anything. They are a week
[sic] race physically and mentally. We are going to continue our
way. We will never be stopped.

>   Anonymous, "Letter to the Editor, on behalf of
>   the Dotbusters," *Jersey Journal*, July 1987

[A] a neighbor of Patel's son, who lived in the Huntsville suburb
of Madison, called police to report a "skinny black guy" who
was "just kind of walking around close to the garage." [Officer
Parker] approached the senior Patel on the sidewalk seeking to
understand what he was doing. Patel only speaks Gujarati and
some Hindi.
    "No English. Indian. Walking," he said [...]
    Police dashcam video captured Parker slamming the
grandfather, then 57, to the ground, leaving him partially
paralyzed.

>   Reuters, 15 January 2016

red
opaque
it thickens

viscid
purple
it gathers

salt to taste
rust to nose

g/ml 1.06

37° C.

/TRINIDAD/INDIA/QUEENS/

the plantations are moving
into the brownstones

a head being swallowed
into its own throat

confetti of bone

when human
     there were three
blood is drawn
     men chasing him
& smeared on a slide
     were all the lights
corpuscles tend to
     on the street shattered
cluster into heaps
     would he have run
like rouleaux of coins
     over the glass
this phenomenon may be
     to reach his house
explained by alteration
     in his own darkness
in surface tension

See Jack
cut sugar
with cane hack
thresh apart jaw
with baseball bat

molasses
falernum
cachaça
our refined blood

"Rishi Maharaj," said
the police, "apologized
repeatedly until
he lost
consciousness"

ऋ ऋषि   "rsh"
to go, to move, to flow

red
pigment
from ore

ground
of ground

a path reddened
along a part
of hair

sRGBB   (227, 66, 52)

CMYKH   (0, 84, 71, 0)

/MUMBAI/ HERTFORDSHIRE/HOBOKEN/

the leafy acres surround
bits of curbside tooth

a skin sprawls out
crawls out of a bar

walks backward home

it is not in its
     there were eleven
nature
     teenagers taunting him
to be exposed
     was he drinking coffee after dinner
to the air
     when they kicked him to the curb
it stands up better
     did the menu have roe
on a panel than on
     slowly roasted
the wall and in time
     his eyeball beaten out
from exposure to air
     by bricks or bats
it turns black
     what does it matter
when it is used
     who you gonna call
& laid on the wall
     dotbusters

See Jack
fry battered cod   सिन्दूर   Navroze Mody
with floured hands   सिंधूर   نوروز [nouˈɾuːz]
break bone   a forehead aflame
with feet and brick   on ghosts   *a new day, of spring anew*

-head

2. An Unbearable Sequence of Happenings

The story reveals the meaning of what
otherwise would remain an unbearable
sequence of sheer happenings.

HANNAH ARENDT, *Men in Dark Times*

It was a nice try. It was a nice move that made the black move to white. A nice move that turned most things away from what they were looking at. Sometimes the way they moved suggested something other than the color of the objects that they looked at. Sometimes these colors turned to ash and then to dust and then they walked away from those colors. In a nice way the walk away had a melody closer to silence than anything else. More than anything it possessed a kind of slow and somber hum. White and blanched like poached eggs in a cream bowl. Slumbering pups overcome by a bitch's thick milk. So much of your eyes are waiting to sup on the right teat. So much of color is waiting. So much of color is in the wait to be seen. One thing radiating points to the other that is not lit.

One thing radiating is in the middle of shade. The shade of the light is uniform and issued to the newly fleshed. To take issue with the midriff of a shade is to force air into a similar stillness. A surplus of inexpensive sky. An expanse of twill which mentions the hands. A flesh of color is the willful opening to some other gesture before a body walks up to you in a warm alley. A flesh is a survey of other black objects coated with lacquer, daubed with plaster, plumped by upholstery. It is the surface to which a name arrives in the eye. The eye in question is at a wake. A name is a hoisted plum in a sulking roasted sow's mouth. This color is a sullied mutton or a beef with someone who owns another name blurred by matted voices calling them into recognition. This is something walking up to you with a face of apology or greeting or wearing or dying in a borrowed trench.

As specific as something appearing in a borrowed trench sits
longer unobserved at a wake. A length of invisibility turns into a
bruise the closer it gets to a fist. Indivisible into parts yet invited
to take part, a waiting body is a puddle forming inside a coat.
Swollen like knuckles. Like red but not red-orange or dark
red or plummy blood pudding, which are shades of a similar
livid lineage. The lineage forms in someone's drowsy wait near
bystanders when the dark breaks in two. It breaks into indefinite
distances of abrupt brightness we call mornings. This body's
color is a startling sleep hung on a hammock between two points:
one known and the other less known. There is an occurrence of
pigment and it suggests a history growing in sand or a method of
preparing lakes or the pliant application of arms to a row. This
body is facing you with a knot of a face made of alum or lye and
wet with linseed oil. That body is folding a glance into a fist-sized
thing to be pocketed by a bystander. This other body is collecting
the toe collecting the finger nail the hanging thing cooling, by the
by. Walking away from this means something about solving water
into fog. To be waded through and not whetted by. To see color is
to apply yourself to a stone like a barber's blade. With a certain
lilt of the neck. A pile of tools and all the lashes in a lather at
this wake for someone's body. A bloom of raspberries wilting in a
tureen once used for serving offal soup.

A bloom of raspberries made an example when, for instance, a
rope touches a nape, when, for instance, the water turns to a boil
and the boil turns back to the water with a questioning glance.
Some examples of instances that are taken when something is
not self-evident like a hanging thing cooling or a rhubarb pie
huddling into the corner of a meshed cupboard. This body's
color is an instance of an example where, for instance, the act of
bringing the witness to the witness stand where the witness sits
instead. This is a confusing proposition of verbs fat with pleasant
symmetry at court. A court takes as evidence the small flush of
violet that grows transparent after the second stoning when blood
ribbons away from the body. Where the blood pools the body
blushes fuchsia then dusky plum draining from an eggy ochre.
In moderation the cause of color is a disagreement between
two similarities. In its basic form the cause of color is the tooth
left behind at the curb. Fusing someone and something color
emerges as a better forgery of resemblance limp and livid at once.
History sleeps in a growing bruise on the ground. Someone is
always begging you not to confound small bits of egg whites with
other white bodies swilling back and forth like irascible pebbles
watching from the bottom of any water.

Someone is always begging you not to shelve this thing at the
helm of being named. On the verge it is something flagged on a
pole and striped with strips of flesh waving or hanging or a pair
of feet not touching the ground when it ought to do otherwise.
Flagged as otherwise color is a swarm of desire formed while
waiting too long in a crowd. Wading far enough in the shallow of
pigment as if a wavelet of a person has its eventual place against
a rock or a shore or a dock of an assembly. An assembly is a
gathering that can carry a body through its due process to an
end. To carry a body to its becoming as carrion by suspending the
weight of a person as strange fruit for the crows to pluck. To carry
on as if color is an area of skin hoisted by a glance or carried like
a chip on the shoulder of mutton. To carry on as if this does not
drown you in weals and welts or turn your chest into a whistle or
a willowy hollow blowing whisht whisht whisht go away.

3. An Unknown Length of Rope

John Singleton Copley, *Watson and the Shark*. 1778.

What I know of the Atlantic is red. What I know of its wetness is blood.

This is a story of three boys, one shark, a length of rope, and many resemblances.

John Singleton Copley's oil painting, *Watson and the Shark*, is a visual report of an incident that did and did not take place.

First, the facts (as they say):

In 1779, Sir Brook Watson is a Tory, 1st Baronet, and in 1796 he is Lord Mayor of London. But, well before that, he is just an orphan cabin boy in Cuba. At this moment in history, Havana is a roiling entrepôt for trading in human slaves. Watson is helping out his uncle whose mercantile trade shares the routes of (and thus moral responsibilities for) the Middle Passage. One cloudy, peach-lit day, Watson is attacked by a shark while swimming in the warm waters of the Havana Harbor (1749). Watson loses his right leg to the shark's attack.

Thirty years after the incident, when he turns forty-four, Watson commissions the American painter John Singleton Copley to memorialize this violent scene, this rescue of a man, this loss of a limb. What interests me is not Watson losing a limb, even though Copley's painting makes this its central problem. What interests me is the painting gaining a black actor during the drafting of the rescue. Of the nine actors in the rescue boat, one is black. But he was not always black. His blackness arrives at the scene of this crisis somewhat belatedly, and yet precedes it.

How?

Brook Watson was fourteen years old when he was attacked by
the shark. The body Copley loans to history, however, is not that
of a fourteen-year-old white child. The painted Watson's thighs
are muscular; the biceps svelte but swollen with effort; the gluteal
curve is meaty, wet; the hamstrings plucked into action. Copley
gives us a Watson that survives. Copley paints for us a man too
young to be the man who commissions Copley and too old to be
the drowning boy. He gives us a body between the drowned and
the saved— the body that can only be witnessed into existence.

How?

The white child rendered by Copley is the symmetrical inversion
of a marble statue of the Borghese Gladiator, discovered in the
early 1600s among the ruins of Emperor Nero's seaside home.
The gladiator is poised, legs apart, defending himself against a
mounting attack with a shield long lost to the elements. In time,
this Greco-Roman warrior would become a model for Copley's
vision of a British politician— Watson. But this time around,
the Borghese gladiator is on his back, reaching up. The arm
that was once raised to shield a face becomes an arm reaching
up to an empyrean God outside the frame. The head and body
seem to send mixed messages: the mouth is agape, gasping, and
desperate; the torso and legs are defiant, impossibly arched. Even
in his drowning, Watson is modeled after a victorious, well-
protected body.

At around the same time, the Borghese Gladiator also became
a model for Australian artist Sydney Parkinson's specimen

engraving of two identical and anonymous aboriginal Australian men pointing a spear and a sword at white men outside the (implied) frame (1770–73). The lost shield, the reaching arm, the improbable weapons— in all cases, this gladiator is stripped and reassembled for his parts. As would be warriors of other kinds— black men and women are used and displaced into confinement in representations they did not permit or are, as we now say, framed.

In this way, a man's flesh and bone become another's— an idea becomes an ideal— and in this way, the flesh and bone of other men become inscrutable, never translated except as deviations from this false original, this forgery. Which brings us to another kind of counterfeit countenance— a face that emerges out of another face. A face that survives another kind of erasure. A face that is a cicatrix. How do we face this face?

How?

Preliminary sketches show that the face of the black sailor throwing a towline into the infested waters to save young Watson used to be the face of a white sailor throwing a towline into the infested waters to save young Watson. The black, white, and red chalk of the preliminary sketches show that Copley intended for all nine actors to be white, including the sailor at the apex of the central tableaux. Somewhere in the drafting, the man became black. He became the apex of the figural triangle and the receded point of the moral triangle— a triangle drawn with three lines to connect a length of rope, a drowning man, and his God.

In Copley's first entry of this painting to the Royal Academy in 1778, its title was:

A boy attacked by a shark, and rescued by some seamen in a boat; founded on a fact which happened in the harbour of the Havannah.

So, that accounts for one boy. And it brings us to our next. The black sailor's face is kith— you may say akin— to one of Copley's earlier studies, *Head of a Negro (Boy)*, which he undertook a year or more before drafting this historical homage to the dramatic scene of thrashing limb, whipping shark fin, and flailing crew. In his earlier study of skull shape and facial structure, a black boy— almost a man, a miraculous survivor of history— emerges from the smudge of a muddy olive coat cut with a flick of white inner shirt. The study is of an open face turning to meet yours. He is caught mid-utterance, or on the brink of a smile, with uncertain eyes.

A critic describes the study of the young black man as an example of Copley caught "in his shirtsleeves, in the midst of things." In the midst of what? We are told: in the midst of encountering a black face in an act of "warm sympathy." The critic interprets this "sympathy" based on the study's lack of ornament, its immediacy, and its absence of elaboration. This critic also suggests that there are three unassailable elements "always present in distinguished portraiture" (in which cache he includes Copley's *Head of a Negro (Boy)*): "a quality of eye— sharpness of observation; a quality of feeling—sympathy; and a quality of hand—style." Whereas the eye and hand are formal means to excellence, here, "a quality of feeling—sympathy" is a moral one. This critic suggests that this personal quality is rare because "no man [artist] is elastic enough to be interested in every stranger that walks into his studio and asks to have his face painted." Copley is an exception in his moral elasticity, perhaps. But perhaps the man he has painted is not a stranger? Perhaps he has not asked to be painted? Perhaps his blackness in the late 1770s or early 1780s expurgates him from the possibility of being a stranger in a white man's household, from the possibility of asking to be painted. He cannot be a subject of this painting. But, as it is a study, he can be its object— he has been studied.

Copley's "warm sympathy" is described again, by the artist's son, when the sketch was for sale:

> 69. Head of a favorite Negro. Very fine—introduced into
> the picture of 'A Boy saved from a Shark' £ 11–11 s

A boy saved from a Shark; a boy drowned in paint. The "favorite Negro" was likely a "favorite family domestic"— and no, the critic never says the word— which may explain the boy's reserve in expression and also the casualness of his displacement. It may explain the child's surprise, the slowly eking smile, and the uncertain, somewhat worried eye.

However, this explains, too, something about how identity is a borrowed thing— first rehearsed through close study and then displaced into new contexts. It explains how artists, like others, learn to mimic what they see and create resemblances as a way of procuring an illusion of a documented incident— of giving an impression of a personal experience.

Watson and the Shark is a benevolent ruse in skilled mimicry.
Copley never visited Havana— he likely borrowed the horizon
and the ship lines from contemporary prints by Canot and
Dumford. He had never seen a shark dead or alive, but he likely
studied a set of jaws disengaged from a cranium. He had never
been part of a rescue in water, so he borrowed from Raphael's
The Miraculous Draught of Fishes. He had never witnessed a
man kill a giant beast, so he mimicked the muscular gesture
and weaponry of St. George slaying the dragon. This is also how
history replicates itself until what little evidence we have of
ourselves is also evidence of how unimaginable we must have
been to those who painted us this way.

Which brings us back to Copley's "favorite negro." His face, now
studied, steadied, and dried, must have moved from Copley's
home into other private homes until it showed up for auction—
again and again. This face hangs now in Detroit, beside one of its
three displacements— one of Copley's three iterations of *Watson
and the Shark*. The year is 1864; the year is 1928; the year is
1951. Copley had dragged a man out of his study and placed him
in one of his own, at the scene of crisis— as the visual apex of
the rescue of a white man.

How?

Does this displacement bear witness to Copley's brush or
his moral imagination— or, the bereavement of both? To
his sympathy or to his appropriation? Perhaps he needed to
fabricate a black body in the Caribbean and he owned one in
Massachusetts he could use. Or, perhaps this "favorite domestic"

of the Copley household was used as the unwitting emblem of the Tory cabinet— a 'favorite export'? Did Watson borrow a colony slave to loan a point to British abolition?

& now the yellow harbor recedes as the foreground deepens into emerald pith.

& here the rescue boat floats in the midriff of the painting— a middle passage between shore and shark. The darkest man is just before dawn.

& here our black sailor precedes even himself in this scene of witness. The white man overboard, the black man in the craft. The year is 1749; the year is 1778.

& here, we are in the same boat. A pale, fleshy pink scarf muffles the line between beige tunic and black face. A pale, fleshy hand blots the line between the domestic laborer and the imagined sailor. Clocks unwind, time turns tables.

& here his head is bent toward water, intent on the shocked and gaping face of the drowning man.

In the process, the black sailor loses his own neck— it becomes a casualty of visual perspective and moral concern— to the act of doubled witness. In contrast, our named victim, Watson, has his neck arched back, his marble clavicles flanking a proud Adam's apple as he stares back in horror from the sea into the sky. In this séance between civility and Christianity, the victim is the medium par excellence.

But what do we glance away from in order to watch this staring match? What else is drowned in this drowning?

How?

Slave ships crossing the Atlantic often used African slaves as human bait— both alive and dead— to troll for sharks that would swarm the slave ship marauding for human remains. Slave ship captains counted on these swarms to terrorize both the slaves and the seamen. As Robert Hayden witnesses that history, he sees "sharks following the moans the fever and the dying"; he sees "horror" as the "compass rose." Like many of us globalized brown walkers— us cosmopolitans; us non-resident so-and-so's; us non-resident jet-setter settlers— the sharks too changed their migratory patterns and followed the slaves across the Atlantic, along a dotted line of corpse and carrion. And when the sharks came to our shores, what hairy legs did they sprout to walk among us? And what fins did we carve to swim beside them?

What I know of the Atlantic is red. What I know of its wetness is blood.

& here we have, instead, Watson— waving and drowning— like so many African children and women and men must have done before being drawn up from the ocean. Nothing more than a pair of heels tied with rope.

& here in Havana is the towline fed into the water by the black sailor, holding his gaze firm and the looped rope loose. His left wrist holds a limp ellipse the size of a man's head. His other hand

is extended, brotherly and forward, to the deadly damp and, also,
sideways to steady his own body against the waves.

& here in Boston, when Copley first called his "favorite Negro"—
he must have been pulled from— what was it— the polishing
of silver, the heaving of logs, the cleaning of boots, the washing
of soot from the irons, the lathering of suede, the stacking of
luggage— and bid sit as duty— for his head— he must have been
pulled from a line. Of duty. As favorite.

So, that accounts for the second boy. And it brings us to our
third.

How?

Salt. Linseed oil. Pigment. Soap. How does one displace what
one has learned of blackness at home, what one has studied of
it— the calm replacement of a face, the patient re-coloration of a
pair of hands— while rendering a catastrophe at sea? What other
catastrophes might Copley have painted over with this face? How
much seawater would it take to wash his hands of this?

When Copley's *Watson and the Shark* was first exhibited in
London, reviewers chaffed at how inert and paralyzed the black
sailor appeared, how detached.

They said:

> *It would not be unnatural to place a woman in the attitude
> of the* black; *but he, instead of being terrified, ought, in our*

opinion, to be busy. He has thrown a rope over to the boy. It is
held, un-sailor like, between the second and third fingers of his
left hand, and he makes no use of it.

They said: He should have chosen better between keeping busy
and being terrified.

They said: He had been given too much rope.

& did it— this black man's face applied to a white sailor's
body— resemble something else black and idle? Something to be
corrected into obedience— into a better use for a rope?

& how might they have used it?

List some uses for rope.

There are no formal statistics for the number of lynchings that
took place in the United States before 1892. There is more than
a century of undocumented and unnumbered lynchings between
Copley's painting of *Watson and the Shark* and the moment when
the Tuskagee Institute begins its records. In 1959, when the
Institute published the last annual report, the number of deaths
caused by lynching in the United States was 4,733. This included
one from 1955: "a Negro who was beaten, shot to death, and
thrown into a river at Greenwood, Mississippi."

Emmett Till, like the drowning Watson, was fourteen years old.

& here again, in the water, inches ahead of the shark's engorged and hungry mouth, is the floating end of the rope thrown by the black sailor— with the face of a nameless boy. The rope's end makes a casual loop, a preemptive halo around Watson's head. It is a lifeline, an umbilicus not yet wrapped around a neck. The rope is a partial ampersand near Watson's head and neck. This is a conjunction that unties other conjectures between ropes and necks— waters, rivers, oceans, and Brooks. Where one ends and the other begins is a history of so many left arms towing the righteous rescues of the wrong bodies.

4. A LAUNDRY LIST

How are we to punish our [Indian] servants when we have no hold either on their minds or bodies?—when cutting their pay is illegal, and few, if any, have any real sense of shame. The answer is obvious. Make a hold. [...] To show what absolute children Indian servants are, [the author] has for years adopted castor oil as an ultimatum in all obstinate cases, on the ground that there must be some physical cause for inability to learn or to remember.

> FLORA ANNIE STEEL AND GRACE GARDINER,
> *The Complete Indian Housekeeper and Cook* (1888)
>
> A book dedicated to "The English Girls to Whom Fate May Assign the Task of Being House-Mothers in Our Eastern Empire"

On April 13, 1919, British Indian Army soldiers under the command of Brigadier-General Reginald Dyer opened fire on an unarmed gathering of men, women, and children picnicking in an enclosed urban garden called the Jallianwala Bagh. This garden is located in Amritsar, India. Amritsar is home to the Sikh holy site The Golden Temple and the Sikh parliament. During the massacre, the firing lasted about 10 minutes. 1650 rounds were fired. 33 rounds per British soldier. There were at least 400 fatalities and 1500 wounded Indians. The urban garden was bounded on all sides by houses and buildings and had few narrow entrances, most of which were kept permanently locked. Since there was only one open exit, except for the one already blocked by armed British troops, people desperately tried to climb the walls of the park and fell to their death. Many jumped into a well inside the compound to escape from the bullets.

Later, rescuers said that 120 corpses were plucked out of the well.

THE FOLLOWING IS A SPECULATIVE LAUNDRY LIST OF OUTFITS
LEFT BEHIND BY CORPSES AT THE 1919 JALLIANWALA BAGH
MASSACRE IF ALL VICTIMS WERE FEMALE AND BRITISH, INSTEAD
OF INDIAN WOMEN, MEN, CHILDREN, AND INFANTS

6000 Calico nightgowns not stained with mud
6000 Silk or wool nightgowns not covered in blood
6000 Calico combinations not damp with well water
6000 Merino vests not splattered with blood
6000 Spun silk vests not stained by rust
6000 Trimmed muslin bodices not ripped by gravel
6000 Calico slip bodices not shredded by thorns
12000 Paris tan stockings not smeared with mud
12000 Lisle thread stockings not speckled with blood
6000 Strong white petticoats not drenched in well water
6000 Lace trimmed petticoats not splotched by clay
2000 Flannel winter petticoats not dripping with well water
3600 Cotton pocket-handkerchiefs not specked with burrs
2000 Evening handkerchiefs not stained by loam
2000 Winter morning dresses not rent by gravel
2000 Summer afternoon linen dresses not torn by thorns
1000 Pairs of leather riding boots not splattered with blood
2000 Tennis dresses not ripped in flight
6000 Summer tea gowns not ripped in flight
1000 Riding habits not ripped in flight
1000 Sun jackets not ripped in flight
1000 Ulster capes not ripped in flight
2000 Sunshades not ripped in flight
1000 Mackintosh jackets not ripped in flight
2000 Pairs of Mackintosh boots not shot through
1000 Pairs of tennis shoes not shot through
2000 Pairs of evening dress shoes not shot through
4000 Pairs of house shoes not shot through
2000 Pairs of work and gardening shoes not shot through

The stockings would have been neither open-work nor black in color, the dresses would have been of washing material and of the sort requiring little starch. Summer cashmeres, delaines, and washing silks would have been suitable, as would have been tweeds and warm shrugs. Gloves would have been rolled up in flannel and bottled in prune jars to keep them from becoming soggy in the humidity, along with the flowers, the ribbons, and the neck scarves. Leather goods would have been wiped weekly and the dresses aired. Needles would have been sealed in court-plaster and camphor would have been added to all chests to keep away mold. Gauze and tulle dresses would have been disastrous, as the damp makes them drop to pieces, as the damp makes them drop to pieces, as the damp makes them drop to pieces.

SALT

Some say that if we eat of your salt and drink of your water, we can never become enemies. And yet from the sweat and blood we have spilled, some others have dredged their salt and drawn their water.

SALT

it grows from ground
water—saltier than sea
—saltier than sweat—it grows
when the sun beats down—turns
earth to salt turns sweat to rupees
it grows from the ground
fields of white
funeral flowers
for the ones who
harvest them

SALT

in the crease
between pit and arm
rings damp on
a hundred dark
boughs swinging
in the bus
going home—they were
going home to wash
salt from the words
you had given them
in exchange for
their word—they were
eating salt from the earth
earning salt from their brows
taking salt back
on their backs

SALT

—look at our house
we spend eight months
here every year
this is the mud
in which we live—

VAJIBHEN KOLI, a laborer in
the salt-pans of Gujarat, as
told to Suzanne Goldenberg
of *The Guardian*

SALT

In 1998, a cyclone off the coast of Gujarat
took them for what they took
from the coast took them
for what the contract took from
their backs turned
to the water their faces
bent to salt flats
their bodies red pillars
turned to salt
between sand and sky
white and white

SALT

her threadbare sari was the last
flag of a tribe
surrendering to a debt
owed to nature built
by the IMF

rupee, dinar
euro, dollar
harrow, horror

SALT

a cyclone off the coast of Gujarat
killed thousands of salt workers
who earned 350 rupees (£5) a week

In 1998, £5 could buy

1. _____
2. _____
3. _____
4. _____
5. _____
6. _____
7. _____
8. _____
9. _____
10. _____
11. _____
12. _____
13. _____
14. _____
15. _____
16. _____
17. _____
18. _____
19. _____
20. _____

SALT

—yes, most of the workers were illiterate and too poor to own a radio—
they had no news of the impending cyclone—there
was an allusion to a newspaper report—contractors, eager
to rake in profits, kept workers in the dark—
—working during the approaching
storm—

SALT

after the eight hundred
dead returned to the shore
bloated beaten spun
pebbled flesh—uncountable
they said, the underwriters
no, we didn't take them down
the names—the migrants
they keep coming
and going who keeps
accounts—the migrants
no, we couldn't pull them out
in time

SALT

—we have a headcount
of animals—lions and tigers—but
—we can't count our own people

ACHYUT YAGNIK, a social activist, on
the Gujarat Cyclone, category 03A

SALT

they told us not
to eat meat drink
toddy comb our hair
facing the east shave
our hoary faces raise
from the bed the dead
their feet pointing
south—they told us
to pull salt
from our mouths
draw ten grams from our blood
where it had already
drowned, bloomed grey
and mute in warm waters

SALT

look at them அம்மா here
they have gathered looking back
at you look at them *appa* there
their hands marked on each palm
their own names
written in salt அண்ணா *akka* they
have scattered in the sand
look at them before the sea
comes back

SALT

your body cannot make salt

it must be offered to you
& taken into your body
through your mouth
& into your life
so you can live

it is a kind of kith—

kith cleaned your teeth, kith relieved your tired feet, kith
soothed your bee stings, kith treated your mosquito bites, kith
eased your sore muscles, kith sloughed off your dry skin, kith
singed off your old tattoos, kith extinguished your grease fires,
kith cleaned soot from your chimneys, kith kept your flowers
from wilting, kith held your silk flowers straight, kith protected
your patios from weeds, kith killed your poison ivy, kith kept
your windows frost free, kith de-iced your sidewalks, kith
deodorized your shoes, kith tanned your leather, kith kept water
in your cells, kith sent messages from your nerves, kith boiled
your water, kith peeled your eggs, kith poached your eggs, kith
prevented them from browning, kith shelled pecans, kith washed
spinach, kith prevented sugaring, kith crisped your salads, kith
boiled your potatoes, kith cleaned your greasy pans, kith cleaned
your stained cups, kith cleaned your ovens, kith deodorized
your refrigerators, kith freshened your coffee, kith seasoned
your poultry, kith removed pinfeathers, kith cleaned tarnished
silverware, kith brightened copper pans, kith scrubbed your
coffee pots, kith removed onion odors from your hands, kith
unclogged your sink drains, kith brightened your cutting boards,
kith scrubbed off dried-on egg, kith prevented mold from taking
over, kith prevented food from sticking, kith whipped your egg
whites, kith kept those white peaks stiff, kith kept your milk
fresh, kith set your jellies, kith polished your brass candlesticks,
kith scrubbed your wicker baskets, kith cleaned greasy rugs,
kith extended your broom's life, kith removed wine stains from
sweaters, kith pulled rings from the mahogany, kith bleached
sweat stains, kith removed blood stains, kith whitened whites,
kith purified your steel, kith scrubbed your fish tanks, kith made
your plastics, kith refined your petroleum, kith preserved your
fish, kith illuminated your purples, kith was worth your gold,
kith was your tax, kith was your offering to god, and so with kith
you gargled your throat and fell asleep with kith in your mouth.

SALT

they didn't have radios
they did not receive word
they were washing
the salt off your word
when it came
when nobody told them
of the storm hurling towards
their children their—

                                        father mother look—
                                        your *us*
                                        includes this

                                        this too is your blood
                                        —is salted kin

SALT

those of us who have stared into sunsets
& those of them who have gone blind from the sun

those of us who have scrubbed our skin with salt
& those of them who have lost limbs to its sting

SALT

kith
those of us who rub salt
into the wounds
of those of them

kith
fleeing
in ships
from a land
filling
with salt water

kith
washing our hands
with fresh water

kith
mining dollars elsewhere
in memory of _____, _____,
_____, _____, _____,
_____, _____, _____,
_____, and _____, _____,
_____, _____, _____,
_____, _____, _____,
and _____, _____, _____,
_____, _____,
_____, _____, _____,
_____, _____, and _____,
_____, _____, _____,
_____, _____, and other kith.

SALT

in a bowl on the rice in a pot beside the aluminum tumblers
in the pan on a field under the feet on your dark hands
in those white palms in between water and earth on your feet
under the sun in the ocean
under the ground in a ward on a pyre
  you were burning
  yours were burning
  your whole lives
to bring salt to our tables to our altars to our banks
from other banks

SALT

it is impossible
to speak of salt
with my mouth full

SALT

—listen
there is just one thing you need
to remember—
about us—
when we die
and put our dead bodies on the fire, our hands and feet don't burn—

VAJIBHEN KOLI, a laborer in
the salt-pans of Gujarat

SALT

because their feet grind into the saltmarsh
because their ankles grind into brine
because their calves grind to a halt over time
because salt cures flesh
when it is set on fire
in a funeral pyre
it does not burn

it does not burn
and so kith arrives
and so kith collects these legs
and so kith buries these legs
in a grave
filled with salt

as told to a reporter
for *The Hindu*,
29 January 2013

SALT

on the 13th day

mourners should bathe
in fresh water

mourners should offer witnesses
from their homes in some small portion
sesame seeds
clothing
gold
silver
ghee
earth
salt

Salt has been grown along the west coast of India (the Rann of Kutch) for over 5,000 years. From at least 1759, the British East India Company charged exorbitant taxes for growing, harvesting, and transporting salt drawn from Indian lands. It secured the British monopolies through intimate, elemental scenarios and cost Indians millions of pounds sterling, despite loud and dire protests.

During the years I have lived in the United States, one of the most well known stories about kith has been about Mahatma Gandhi's Dandi March (the *Salt Satyagraha*)— his campaign of tax resistance and non-violent protest against persistent British colonial presence. As part of systematic action towards *swaraj* ("self-rule"), Gandhi broke the salt laws by marching to Dandi, in the Indian state of Gujarat.

On 6 April 1930, when he reached Dandi, Gandhi said a prayer, scooped up some earth laden with the rich mineral and declared: "With this, I am shaking the foundations of the British Empire." He then boiled this earth in seawater and produced illegal salt. Inspired by this act of elemental disobedience, tens of thousands of Indians took part in ripple actions that resulted in the arrest of over 80,000 civilians. And this drew the world's attention to the desperation and resistance of an enslaved and colonized people.

Since then, salt has remained a symbol of liberation, defiance, and survival for kith.

And yet, in the very state where Gandhi symbolically separated salt from earth, and Indian from colonized civilian, thousands of Indians remain enslaved to salt production through the persistence of salt monopolies and vice-tight contracts of indentured labor. Through elaborate financial schemes that favor contractors and unregulated incentives for global enterprises, saltpan laborers are caught between the teeth of debt and work for negligible wages in neo-colonial conditions. Without protective clothing or footwear, they suffer extraordinary occupational hazards and remain some of the least protected civilians in India, entrapped at the deadly intersection of poverty, illiteracy, and migrancy.

Daya Ranto, a 48-year-old father of three, told *The Telegraph*: "We produce the most important food ingredient, but we are never given importance. Poverty is our fate." And the fate of the 200,000 salt miners along the Rann of Kutch is preserved in salt. Ambu Patel, a social activist, laments: "There is a saying here that if you're a saltpan worker, you have three ways to die: first gangrene, second TB (tuberculosis), or third blindness. In every house, people die this way."

As a metaphor, salt helped kith win independence; as a commodity, it has caused others to remain enslaved. Both these stories should become equally well known.

If salt can wear away at iron and stone, it can wear away at human flesh and bone.

there is always
more where
this comes from
like kith

like salt
kith preserves
the parts of us
that refuse
to burn
in a pyre

KIN

PARENT PATTERNS

1995

"Señorita, bade bade deshon mein aisi choti choti baatein hoti rehti hain."

"Señorita, in big-big countries such small-small things keep happening."

> SHAH RUKH KHAN
> in *Dilwale Dulhaniya Le Jayenge*

2015

"Señorita, bade bade deshon mein … er … you know what I mean … "

> PRESIDENT BARACK OBAMA
> on Indo-American relations at Fort Siri, New Delhi

vy do yoo stand
neeyar the vindow
verr yoo will
undowtubbly
catch one coldu

vy do yoo stand
neeyar that boyy
he is defeenately
going to make yoo
failu maths nextu time

vy are yoo looking
at me like one
Christmas tree
with all the bulbs
in yoover face like that

vy do yoo insist
on yelling and yelling
about small small
things like this and that

vy must yoo always
do this to me in the
yeevenings right before
yoover father comes home

vy is ess oh are are vy
so hard for yoo to
ess aye why

FAMILY PORTRAITS

When the photographer came home, the children ran screaming and hid in the servants' skirts. The men lit cigarettes and tugged on their cuffs, walking to the settees and whistling the dogs into the frame.

The women? The women were nowhere to be seen.

A.

Kanyakumari District, Tamil Nadu, India.
21 May 1991

I am 8 years old and waking up to my mother whispering in
my ear: "I'm going to tell you something. When you wake up
everyone will be talking about this. Rajiv Gandhi has been
assassinated. You don't have to wake up right away."

When Rajiv Gandhi was pausing to hug children on his campaign
trail, Thenmozhi Rajaratnam, a young girl, had walked up to
him with 700 grams of RDX explosives snug under her clothes.
They said she was a girl soldier for the Liberation Tigers of Tamil
Eelam (Tamil Tigers).

For days after that, the photographic aftermath of the
assassination sprawls on miles of inky front pages. The *Hindu* and
Dinakaran are damp with splayed bodies edged in neon purple
or blackened by the RGB rush or grainy and mealy in black and
white. Rubber chappals are scattered everywhere— everywhere
unpaired. Many things are without context or continuity. Necks
end where they shouldn't. Ankles on their own.

I hold the front page up to my face framed by two thick black
braids. I hold the Reuters photographs one inch away from my
eyes. When no one is looking, I try to peer into the holes in
the bodies— peer sideways into the lacerations. I try to match
scattered body parts from different newspapers; I beg my older
cousins to buy the evening post, the morning post, the socialist
post. They buy me rose milk at the newspaper stand. I insist,
pressing the translucent broadsheets to the TV screen waiting for
the right thigh or left foot to line up. The dots are disconnected;
the crayon is clutched.

Buffalo, New York, United States of America.
10 April 2014

This is the first instance of ink on newsprint that helps me understand color in the United States twenty-three years later. Pages and pages of bodies fallen like limp confetti and colored in leaky ribbons of soy inks tinted prussian blue (iron, carbon, nitrogen), cadmium yellow (cadmium and sulfur), and chrome green (chromium, oxygen). Titanium white. Painted humans. A headline about a headless nation.

Months later, these newspapers carrying news of the assassination would be used to line kitchen shelves and altars; to package dried anchovies and sugar; to wrap fried bananas and crisp tapioca fritters. Vegetable oil glossed the corpses and darkened the dead. These images were then placed in picnic baskets, grocery bags, and lunch bags— with the history books, protractors, and compasses. This is how the photographs traveled. The camera and its catastrophic trail. The photographs first made sure that we were always at some stranger's funeral, and then, that we fell asleep at the wake.

Singapore, Singapore.
6 September 2015

Dear Thenmozhi,

At the scene of the assassination, you were wearing a bright
garland of kanakambaram in your hair— *Crossandra
infundibuliformis*— firecracker flowers. They are named for their
seedpods, which explode after the flowers wither and scatter their
seeds to the land on which they die.

When my mother woke me up that morning in 1991, she did not
tell me that a child had done this. She did not want me to know
that a girlchild, meant for a life of well-packed school bags and
hot lunches, had carried history in her luggage and unpacked
her grief with such sound and certainty. She did not want me to
know a history so uncontainable, so untenable that it flew from
your bones, rent your spine, severed your head, broke our vision
of girlchildren leaning in to press puffy stickers on pencil cases—
divide six by two. You must have been too old for that— too
hungry, too angry.

They did not explain to me how a child on her way into a sari
shedding ribbons stepping out of skirts and socks could walk
into the arms of a man she barely knew and burn his flesh by
striking herself against her own history like a match. Thenmozhi,
your name means *honeyed tongue* and your language was a
phosphorescence born of friction between body and nation. They
should have said it then— that your tongue was mine; that our
lands were twins separated at birth; that your body had never
been yours to keep.

B.

Kanyakumari 1993// Philadelphia 2006

sweat/ man/ sarong/ clod
lunge/ cigarette/ cur/ road
mange/ whiff/ yellow/ blur
angle/ gate/ thigh/ dust
hollow/ tar/ crease/ gutter

& there?

> : *there* an arrangement of spines as
> a derangement of girls as an arranged
> marriage as a lone stranger as one
> anger as a neon strangle as onward as if an
> arrangement of spindles as if an estrangement
> of wombs as if a harangued
> marring as if a marauder
> stronger as if one stranger as if none
> wrangle and onward as if this was an arrangement
> of splinters as well as a branch wrenched
> from rooms as well as _____ was hanged
> for marrying as well as a hunger breaches or
> renders strangers as wells do girls as well as
> fragile bones hold bangles around them glass and all
> *yes, glass and all*

\twelve pews \two rings \one sermon

Trichy 1989// Seattle 2007

ribbon/ bonbon/ bib/ table
pig/ rub/ slate/ tooth
milk/ tug/ block/ plate
cud/ bed/ teat/ elbow
blood/ tussock/ chalk/ bog

& there?

: *there* a framed child against a steel
beam against a man tamping rails or paving
across the bricks racked high against
cramped prams lined against throngs
of brown arms ramming against rain and again
a framed hide aghast their street bears upon
the men stamping over hair and plaits
sprawl over the rickshaw tracks those small
eyes upon wet bramble upon limb under
the tram rambling her nerves
and again _____'s shins like flints
in framed rain
a pint of flesh against white hail and one little
two little three little things watching
twin palms holding the bars rust and all
yes, rust and all

\four wheels \six teaspoons of sugar \one torn lip

C.

HL190.1
yes, and their husbands promised to send them passports and
visas. but they never came back. so pregnant they were. don't
know how they managed at the wells.

HL191.20
this one was the daughter of a set of fingerprints.

HL220.34
this one we once saw again, but we couldn't remember what it
was that she had had.

HL193.0
yes, I don't remember this.

HL194.02
he was the first to have a mustache. he was the last to die.

HL205.0
they were always yelling for no good reason this and that all the
time who knows. those people were all the same.

HL187.31
why would we care? I didn't plant them— she said I did, but
I didn't. well. anyway no one knows how they started growing

but someone must have watered them with water drawn from
somewhere I suppose everything needs someone.

HL188.0
no, they also did this to children. but that has probably stopped
now. everyone is going to college, educated. no, no.

HL191.0
this one, yes, the son of the goldsmith— they said anyone who
married him died after giving birth to a pair of crow's wings.
maybe two women. why would I lie.

HL203.2
it is possible that he is still living but I am not sure anyone
would know. he had a staircase in his house. more than we had.

HL207.40
we went here to dig the well and they closed it up after the
second one fell in. the hibiscus looked like wax that year. white
and red. the children after school would light them on fire. that
year all the wells dried up. except the one in our village.

HL208.40
this is the fence— yes.

FOREIGN TERMS

Foreign words and phrases that have not yet
become Anglicized (not found in *Webster's*) are
italicized on first appearance in text and legends.

National Geographic Style Manual,
"Foreign Terms"

[A]lmost all absurdity of conduct arises from the
imitation of those whom we cannot resemble.

SAMUEL JOHNSON,
Rambler No. 135 (2 July 1751)

EXERCISES

IN

ENGLISH AND TAMIL.

Can you speak English?

நீ இங்கிலீசுப் பாஷை பேசக் கூடுமா?

I can speak a little.

நான் கொஞ்சம் பேசுவேன்.

I can speak better than I can read.

நான் வாசிக்கிறதிலும் பேசுகிறது திறம்.

I know a few words.

எனக்குச் சில சொற்கள் தெரியும்.

I cannot speak but I can read.

எனக்குப் பேசத் தெரியாது வாசிக்கத் தெரியும்.

I have bought a grammar.

நான் ஒரு இலக்கணப் புத்தகங் கொண்டேன்.

Who can teach me to read?

எனக்கார் வாசனைப முக்கக் கூடும்?

Do you know any one who teaches English?

இங்கிலீசுப் பாஷை படிப்பிக்கிற யாதொருவரை அறிவீரா?

There is an English school in town.

பட்டினத்தில் ஒரு இங்கிலீசுப் பள்ளிக்கூடமிருக்கின்றது.

The master is clever.

அந்த உபாத்தியார் மேத்தக்கெட்டிக்காரன்.

I also can teach English.

நானும் இங்கிலீசு படிப்பித்தக் கூடும்.

---

from *Phrase Book: Or, Idiomatic Expressions in English and Tamil. Designed to assist Tamil Youths in the Study of the English Language.* American Mission Press, Jaffna. 1848

My mother, given more to strong opinions than a strong stomach, was vomiting when they drew me up from her. Without knowing it, she had birthed an Indian writer who would become an American writer writing in Singapore.

My— we say என்னுடைய— 'ennudaya' (which is to say: *with me*; mine).

My mother doesn't read Indian writers because she feels that the peacock-to-people ratio in the fictional Indias *far* exceeds the ratios likely in the real India. She feels this way too about mentions of pickles, mangoes, neem trees, and the entire figurative spectrum of dusk to caramel to coconut husk: "We are a People, not desert or landscape," she insists. I'm less sure about the difference. Something in her curdles away in disgust when she sees any India that is hers alone to love become beloved to those who have no right to love it. Something in her cringes at spectacles. Especially spectacles crowded with bodies and memories like ours.

Her declarations would rupture into breakfast like an overheated Velveeta box— I'd recommend a Rushdie or a Desai and she'd point to her own mother, standing (always) about two feet away: "I have her. I don't need novels. I don't need histories written for white people without passports." Hers is an affectionate and possessive critique of representation; mine is a distanced and scholarly one. Perhaps this is what one calls a generational difference— how much we care about *how* we are wronged.

For years, this has been my own beloved brand of critique against Orientalism— a dire warning against self-exoticization, against writing as explanation. Our conversations about this are not long— my mother doesn't always converse, she *tells* you— but those conversations have been an important part of why and how I write for American audiences, often white audiences.

"Never become a jingle of anklets or a profound sunrise in a colonizer's imaginary. Make sure you remain there like an immovable boulder. We've moved enough."

My mother and I tried on these opinions while waiting in endless queues and cramping up in waiting rooms in Baltimore and San Francisco; Singapore and Chennai; at airports and DMVs; at immigration offices and human resources cubicles; at Principals' offices and holy-communion lines. We'd shift our weight and slap a foot awake and continue to discuss the fine line between expressing oneself and explaining oneself to my largely white audience in the United States. The difference, it seemed, was a matter of how much I cared about being understood. Whether I cared about being known by my readers. And whether being known is worth very much.

here, the habit of tucking her hand into the folds of a sari— first her mother's and then her own

My mother and I would fill out folders of immigration paperwork
on Sunday afternoons, explaining ourselves to officials and
strangers:

Have you or have you not been accused of a Crime?

*Do you intend to remain in the United States beyond
the time period ascribed by your H1-B VISA and/or the
termination of the H1 holder's employment?*

A hundred times a month, we wrote out our own names in carbon
copy— in duplicate and triplicate. Finely printing the letters into
those pink boxes. And so it was that we multiplied ourselves into
bureaus and folders, into hard drives and databases. We wrote for
them our names again and again. We wrote our way into staying
in this country.

After nearly a decade of writing my way into a home, I slowly
began to unitalicize my language. To italicize was a way of
explaining— it meant, *Sorry you don't understand this word I'm
using even though everyone I love understands it. Here, let me
help you.* It was a way of looking at an audience that I knew could
not look back. I began to write in an English that others had
borrowed from us for centuries. I have refused to remain foreign
in a language that is as much mine as it is yours.

~~candy, ginger, teak, toddy, vetiver, pariah~~

CANDY. GINGER. TEAK. TODDY, VETIVER, PARI___

PARIAH. an outcast. From the Tamil "paṟaiyar" பறையர்
or Malayalam "paṟayan"— "drummer"

An outcast drummer. He does not italicize his drums.

& so I began this manuscript. & so I made of poetry something
other than an explanation
        — of an "us" you couldn't know
         — of kith unitalicized.

This is an argument, as it always has been, for writing what I know alongside what I don't yet know; for speaking in languages borrowed from ancestors and for learning languages that serve not commerce but conscience; for continuing the work of culture from mouth to mouth. We are not parrots or mynahs that mimic borrowed human speech while in captivity, as they claimed. We are lyrebirds and magpies who borrow bars from what they hear and remain free in the wild.

A is for Ammani

My mother has always claimed that she doesn't have a name
of her own. Despite having three. She was named Cecily
Lourdammal Simon and then nicknamed Ammani by her kith.
Her first, Cecily, is the name of her maternal grandmother— a
soft and chalky plinth of woman with a genuine affection for
yearlings and weaner calves, often wrapped in gauzy cottons (like
she was bandaged) in photographs. Her second, Lourdammal, is
borrowed from her paternal grandmother— a fierce and unlikely
politician who changed the fate of fisheries (and fishermen) in
Tamil Nadu and an embroiderer of pastoral landscapes. Her third
and familial, Ammani, is a surrogate name given to her after
her own father's sister died in infancy and had no more use for
it. Elsewhere in India, Ammani is what you call anything under
three feet wearing pigtails, carrying a paper cone of peanuts.
But a nickname is also a nick. So, a later Ammani, the ghost of
a ghost, would be called by her late father's last name and her
husband's middle one.

B is for Buhari's Pistabar Chocobar Ice Cream

My father, who everyone calls Victor, has no name in particular
that he (or anyone else) could settle on. Victor has a habit of
talking about dessert. Dessert is always a thing we don't have.
In our homes, it was absent even when we were eating it. It was
absent— *das Ding*— because it was *not* the dessert he did *not*
get to eat when he was little. My father's digestive history is an
obstacle course made entirely of glistening chocolate snares and
marzipan bear-traps. One must make it through these to get to
the ascetic narrative of gruel and hard work in order to arrive
at The Man. The Man and his Sweets: An Immigrant History in
Borrowed Half-Cups of Sugar.

My father, his square palms to the round steering wheel of the
Toyota Camry, is John Victor Pudota— a man whose middle
name became his first and my last.

We drive along the California coast, John Steinbeck's Monterey
flashes by; slick black seals and sea lions defecate competitively
with the cormorants, pelicans, and ashy petrels on Bird Rock,
which is a live guano impasto. "Did I ever tell you about
Buhari's ice cream?" He ekes open a milky bloom of Chennai in
the greywacke and shale flanks of Route 101. "I tell you. It was
the best ice-cream. There was this guy— this skinny guy, dark,
like one I don't know what— wearing one lungi, who would
cycle over with an icebox of Buhari's ice cream screaming in
one skinny voice: '*Pistabar! Chocobar! Ice Cream! Buhari's Ice
Cream!*' I've never eaten ice cream as tasty as that."

And then, (and this has happened for thirty years) my mother, invariably asleep in the backseat— lulled by the Toyota pulsing like her childhood's Ambassadors thrumming through the tropical steppes of Amritsar— will wake up for long enough to say: "And they had the best gulab jamuns too." At which point, my eternally quiet grandmother would emerge out of her salt-and-pepper chignon long enough to say: "Nowadays where do we have that nowandall, no?"

"And only 5 paise!" she'd add, before disappearing into the blue-bright scenery of Route 101.

Sometimes kith is just small-boned monologues held in the cradle of a road trip— an American tradition with other stories of other others.

C is for Comorin and not Chutney

I am not allowed to talk about chutney here because of an
unspoken agreement I have with kith about the signals we send
out about our origins. Well-mannered Indian writers don't let
their origins hang out like some prolapsed hem. One must leave
an impression without dropping calling cards, without pissing on
all the trees. We are of the opinion that when we say chutney, you
think of "chutney" and you are *veryvery* wrong in doing so.

So, C is for Comorin. This is where my grandmother sped from
fetus to newly married in eighteen years like a compact Fiat at
break-neck speed in the Kanyakumari district. Here, three types
of soil swirl in the coastal eddies— a sandy gold from the Bay of
Bengal, a graphite black from the Arabian Sea, and a rusty brown
from the Gulf of Mannar. She would have stood here looking out
to Sri Lanka before they put up the rocks that made the people
afraid of the sea until it came for them and took them back like
so many lovers do. But here she is too, in a Pennsylvania winter,
splinters of light falling at her small soft feet.

Her kith is spun like gold from flax in free WiFi calling and
postage stamps bought in bulk at Costco. Hers is a kith of letters
and engaged lines— of mail lost in wars and telephone poles
shattered by tsunamis.

D is for Dawn

My almost-name. In a fit of national and ethnic pride, my parents, who owe their own names to so many garlanded hagiographies, New Testament anecdotes, and Greek tragedies— John the Baptist, St. Lourdes, St. Cecily, Helen of Troy— decided that their Indian child should have an Indian name: something that was more than a time of day— something less arbitrary than a horizon.

E is for Edlove's Stationery Store

Edlove was a purveyor of rulers and erasers, chocolates and highlighters. He was, in other words, the be-all and end-all of fashion trends in Trichy township if you were between the ages 5 and 10. The 11-year-olds had graduated to sodas and candy cigarettes, leaving kithchildren to suck on scented erasers like perverse pups at some post-apocalyptic teat (Piña Colada Flavor). The 13-year-olds had no use for stationery, having moved on to the trapping of tadpoles and the hunting of gutter-water popsicles. The class hierarchy (that is, scholastic) was clear in those days, and Edlove exploited it like a hard-shelled soft-centered zamindaar of all our earthly desires. The other class hierarchy (that is, capitalistic) was the very thing *Edlove's* helped varnish over, like a crafty blend of diacetyl and beta-carotene on popcorn— we could never believe it was not butter Because Betty Botter Bought a Bit of Better Butter to Make the Bitter Butter Better. Which is to say, Edlove gave me my first taste of the free market.

Edlove was a man with a mole that squatted on his face like an errant peppercorn from his Ernakulum days. Edlove's mole judged schoolchildren and coveted the ten-rupee note tucked into the thick waists of their thin-armed maids. It watched kithchildren as we picked sheets of clipart to cut and paste, literally, with glue made of boiled rice (working class) or syrupy Fevicol (middle class). It watched kithchildren as we ran our fingers on the stacks of Five Star chocolate bars; as we itched the crisping blisters in our dusty knockoff Keds; as we rubbed our eyes with a sleepy abandon known only to smallthings on their way home from school.

Today, as I walk past a stationery mart at the Mall in West Jurong, Singapore, monitored by bored, overglossed teenagers, I scoff at the child-customers allowed to graze without the fear of the surveying Mole. Little do you know, children, the wars that have been fought for your desire for novelty paper clips and lemon-scented freedoms. Ours is the hostile kith of capital— the cartilage that fuses my wallet to my spine, which alters my gait with debt.

G is for Godrej Consumer Products Ltd.

Sometimes kith is a feeling we steal back from product placement. Godrej brand products colonized our regulation township flat— all 400 square feet of it— and in my history of kith, I find myself trying to wrest a home away from the powders and potions and electrical monsters that haunted our small flat. Sitting on kitchen shelves while we slept; peeking from cupboards as I solved sums; droning in our empty houses while we worked to afford them.

Kith keeps meat in Godrej fridges; keeps passports in Godrej steel almirahs; keeps credit ratings high to afford more Godrej more often.

My father's hair (when he still had it) smelled of the floral and vetiver soapiness of Brylcreem. This emulsion of water and mineral oil, sturdied up with beeswax, which scented and disciplined the hair (and hairpieces) of kithmen for decades, was bought by Godrej from County Chemicals at the Chemico Works in Birmingham, England. In this way, the signature jawline and left-hand slow bowl ("The Chinaman" as it was named) of Middlesex cricketer Denis Compton came into our home and endorsed my father's body.

The many pairs of hands that belonged to maternal kith smelled of the juniper green block of soap called Cinthol— another Godrej 'classic'— a lexical blend, I speculate, of cinnamon and menthol. We kept these blocks by wash-basins because they dissolved slowly and lathered vigorously. And because we wash our hands before we eat, our first bites of rice and sambar were also laced with laureth sulfates. In this way, scenes of Vinod Khanna (and his feathered Fawcett) crashing into ocean waves in double-denim outfits, Vinod Khanna riding a glistening stallion in a crisp blue collared shirt, Vinod Khanna slipping into a slick black convertible in a tuxedo came into our home with their own AmeroBritish blend and endorsed our sleepy breakfasts.

Like Rilke's father's hands, those kith-hands too slowly disappear in my own "more slowly disappearing hands" as I type. And the pair I have left here smells of Lifebuoy soap (Unilever)— its carbolic acid and phenol, my poison and comfort. How does one divest kith from the "gush up economics" of the Godrejs and Tatas and Ambanis who became rich while promising us the same? Who remained in India and made us leave kith behind.

H is for Her Hair

In Toni Morrison's *Song of Solomon,* there is a scene in which a grandmother, a mother, and a daughter discuss how Milkman could hate Hagar's (the daughter's) hair— they ask: "How can he love himself and hate your hair?"

Kithwomen could learn something from black women about how a braid can be a chain; how a comb can become a weapon— or— about how a braid can moor us to kith; how a comb makes a part between kith and unkith— follicle by follicle.

Kith hair wraps around the teeth of a comb— cream, gold, and black. Kith hair speckles the sink after a mustache has been trimmed. Kith hair is caught in a drain— our black cord through pipes and pens— ink and blood running through these knotted dark lifelines.

Age 11, Singapore. A Eurasian classmate complains to the teacher that kithchild's hair is too big— that kithchild's curls are blocking the blackboard. Kithchild is sent to the back of the class and stays there until it graduates.

Age 12, Singapore. A Chinese classmate asks kithchild if it ever loses its pencils and erasers in its hair; if it gets tangled up while walking tall under short trees; if it might swing from those branches in case that happens.

Age 13, Singapore. A Malay classmate asks another classmate to leave kithchild alone when kithchild is asked if kith eat lice caught in each other's hair.

Age 14, Singapore. Kithchild cuts off all its hair because it has to play the role of Macbeth in an all-girl production. A Chinese classmate asks with great concern if kithchild is worried that hair now looks like kithman's crotch.

Age 16, Singapore. Kith saves enough money to pay for kithchild to have hair chemically straightened at a salon. The cost is a large fraction of Mother's paycheck earned at an institute for the cultural advancement of kith whose kith arrived as indentured labor almost a century ago. At the salon, kithchild sits with head bowed and eyes red because salon employees are called to look at kith hair. The pointing and the looking. The ways of eyes and fingers that create kith and unkith. And kith looks back at kith sitting in other chairs looking on at kith being looked at. Their heads bowed and eyes red too. With black shrouds around their necks, they are bodiless. Kithchild walks back home, its scalp crusted with blood and hair smelling of formaldehyde. Mother washes pillowcases every other day to remove the blood and stench of change from the house.

Age 38, Baltimore. Mother standing in a PayLess Shoe Store has her thick, waist-long braid touched and pulled by a white woman. Startled, Mother shudders at the compliment. Your people have beautiful hair. My people, Mother learns, do not like to be touched by your people. Kith is born between aisles 8½ and 9.

Age 68, San Francisco. Grandmother standing squarely in her round way and on her own stoop— her hip-length silver hair wild and flying open like the windows of a haunted house on Halloween. "For me, no costume required," she grins at kithchild holding bowl of M&M FunPacks, the autumnal squal turning a corner.

Age 32, Singapore. Kithchild returns to the scene and the same Chinese classmate, now grown, says: "Not bad, you finally learned to do something with your hair."

Kith *had* learned to do something with hair. Kith was born by pulling its hair, braid by braid, from the throats of unkith. Kith was made climbing down its own braid. From her hair we made sails and from her hair we made paper and with a brush of her hair we wrote kith. Kith is untying her braid, link by link, to find another place to become kith without head bowed, without eyes red.

I is for Innie

Kithwomen are divided along color lines. We must first be checked off as "fair," "dark," or "wheatish" in order to be checked out. The ubiquitous product of skinshame— a cream called Fair and Lovely— offers kithwomen a "safe skin lightening technology" while "empowering individuals to Re-script their Destiny." Because skin color is destiny, as Unilever well knows. And that is both fair *and* lovely. As is the destiny of the thousands of Indian workers whose lives have been poisoned by mercury because of the Anglo-Dutch company's use of Kodaikanal, and kithwomen, as its toxic dumpsites. And today, stunned in the bright lights of American Supermarket Individualism, I pick my way through 18 foundation shades— Maybe She's Born With It! Maybe It's A Profitable Biopolitical Caesura Affirmed By Imperialist Expansion!

An early discovery about the disparities of skincolor happened with two pairs of pedal-pushers dropped around two pairs of ankles. Two five-year-old girls mirror each other, pants down, shirts up, guts out. They push their torsos forward until both their belly buttons touch. One has an innie and the other an outtie. They want to fit together; to click into place and form an antenatal union postpartum, years after their separate mothers carried separate fetuses of separate caste and creed— one smeared in holy ash, the other washed in a holy font.

Between her groin and her belly, the slim pale lines showed where her body could fold in two or three, like white edges of surf show us where the wave ends and the ecru shore begins with a spray of down. I pretended that those lines showed us where they had peeled me from her and laid me in the sun to turn brown and laid her in the bed to turn white. We pressed our palms together, clamped our mouths shut and tried to breath through each other's bellybuttons, turning blue from our different browns.

These pale waves that run the length and breadth of all bodies are called Langer's lines— topological contours that tell you how your collagen naturally orients itself and how the skin spreads outwards in waves. In order to discover how skin put itself together, the scientist Karl Langer stuck metal picks in a cadaver and watched for the directions in which skin fell apart.

When our parents carried us back to our separate homes we must have understood how insufficient it was to have just one body— how meager and useless to have just one.

J is for Jarasandha

There once lived a great king whose twin wives could bear him
no children. A wandering sage saw the king's grief and offered
him a magical mango. She who ate the mango would be with
child. As he had two wives, the king cut the mango into two
perfect halves and offered one half to each wife. After nine
months, each wife gave birth to one lifeless half. Horrified,
the king ordered these clots of flesh to be left in the forest. A
wandering demon found the two lifeless halves and cupped one
in each palm. When she brought them together, the two halves
fused and a whole child was made in front of her eyes— the
demon named the child Jarasandha.

Years passed by and this child grew to be an intimidating and
invincible warrior. In a fight with Bhim, an equally invincible
warrior, Jarasandha was ripped in half by his enemy. But, each
time he was ripped apart, his halves found a way to meet up and
become whole. Krishna, who witnessed how Jarasandha's flesh
found its own way back to flesh, motioned to his own cousin with
his fingers: *toss the halves of his body in opposite directions,* he
suggested.

So, when Bhim ripped Jarasandha apart once again, he swung his
left half to the right side of the arena and his right half to the left.
And his body found no way to return to itself.

In the Toronto airport, where I've arrived for a conference, I
watch an older Punjabi lady— made to sit in a wheelchair behind
two lines of customs officials, a security guard, a translator, and

a service-staff member— scream that her son is outside the airport may she please just go tell him she is here she is here she is here please. I stand there holding her hand, my own luggage reluctantly traveling in loops on the belt. Beta— child— she says to me: please tell them my son is here and I am here what is the problem let me go let me go to him.

K is for Kerchiefs

An average eight-year-old is just four feet of sugar, snot, and dirt. I was no exception. The only thing that deviated me from deviling in gutters, ditches, and other muddy crevices was the weekly film screening at a small outdoor theatre with rows of metal folding chairs. When the stony heat of Trichy afternoons broke, they waited, dewy and cold, for our starched pants and pleated skirts. Of the inappreciable gestures of fraternity between family members, one is the flit of hands offering handkerchiefs to the youngest sprout so it could dart about daubing up the dew from the folding chairs. You could watch how the handkerchief travelled, from hand to hand— the mother's, a blue cotton embroidered with freesias; the grandmother's, a butter-colored lace daubed with Vicks VapoRub; the father's, a crisp white wilting after a day at the plant. And you could tell where one family ended and another family began by the journey of the kerchief— from pocket to fist to seat to fist— whose hand it left and to whose hand it returned. In the rows and rows of an *us*, there were the *theys* and *thems* and the *other-ones* loosely threaded together by the scurry of fabric and the pocketing of a now slightly damper handkerchief. These would come out again, invariably, because the feral four feet of sugar, snot, and dirt would collide with a wall or trip on a branch in the mad rush for Intermission samosas and peppermints and would need daubing or bandaging.

Cinema was a civilizing experience for scuff-cuffed and scabby-kneed girls not because of the films, *per se*. Though I did learn much about American families from *Home Alone* and *The*

Exorcist, these were beside the point. In the hushed crackle of a darkening audience and scratchy roll of the opening credits, you learned to whom you belonged— how tribe was invented between the folds of a large, soggy kerchief clutched in a small, grubby fist.

I moved, at 18, from Singapore to Towson, a college town near Baltimore. One afternoon, watching an episode of *The Simpsons* in slowly curdling horror, I picked up the head-bobbing, egg-tongued Apu with a memory of these handkerchiefs and bandaged the crack where every episode broke our migrant lives in two— into set up and punch line. After every freshman party, the slow swirl of warm beer at the bottom of a plastic cup— and in its eddy, the certainty of having failed, repeatedly, to explain away the act of twisting wrong our lives for a joke. Did you hear the one.

L is for LAX to TRV, Economy Class

Whiteness first arrived in a Samsonite suitcase traveling from Sacramento to Trivandrum in 1987 when my Indian-American family had come to visit my Family-family. Whiteness arrived in Baby Auntie's copy of *Glamour* with Cindy Crawford on the cover; her eyebrows were the brushed out wingspan of a pet eagle, its talons grasping an olive branch and arrows, her earrings were drizzled yellow mustard against a dewy hotdog. Whiteness arrived tucked into the silky puckered compartment where Baby Auntie had kept her silky puckered things and the sour hard boiled sweets that made my mouth into a silky puckered thing as I sat on a parapet swinging my legs in skirts the way one is allowed to until one's skirts start filling up with blood. Whiteness arrived as a woman's leg in a red stiletto. It began at a pale, dog-eared knee and ended at a glossy toe and it was wrapped in a champagne-colored nylon stocking. I borrowed the magazine and pressed it to my chest. Later, lying on the terracotta terrace, I placed the cool magazine page on my right leg and closed my eyes. The sun's spangles lifted each eyelash like a curtain that would never again fall on my darkness.

Whiteness wasn't smuggled in— it was given the red carpet. The American dollar arrived that same year. It levitated, scented like cinnamon gum and leather, hot from my Baby Auntie's purse. The budding baby-slumdog-millionaire in me pressed its creased, greasy flatness between its hands in a fawning namaste that still turns my toes numb in shame. In 1987, one US dollar was worth 13 Indian rupees. One of theirs was worth thirteen of ours. Today, one of theirs (of mine) is worth sixty-eight of ours (of theirs).

When my aunt arrived in India, she was a new brand of
Indian— a hyphenated American, as compared to us Standard
Edition Indians, the *mere* Indians of Kipling, of Tagore, of
Merchant Ivory films, of Ben Kingsley wrapped in kadhi being
photographed by Candice Bergen relaxed in khakis, of *National
Geographic*'s sympathetic coverage of our asses hanging low over
all the gutters of your jungle books.

In family photographs, Baby Auntie's hair is an autumnal
bonfire whipped by the wind and her waistline is crimped by
a bright slash of a galaxy I could never reach. Her madras-
checked shift grids her curves— 75% cotton, 25% linen. I squint
around the sparks of her halo and see the other women standing
in dark silhouettes around her— their black hair parted down
the middle, curtly tucked behind the ears, and pulled into
demure braids leading the eye to hips wrapped in four layers of
chiffon or cotton, straddled by my cousins' scabby and ashy legs,
proudly dangling a worn rubber chappal.

The front cover of the *Glamour* magazine that Baby Auntie had
purchased for $1.95 at LAX was advertising "Great Fashion
Buys under $57." In 1987, $57 was ₹741, which would have paid
a month's rent and my school fees. The "rupee" derives from
the Sanskrit rupya, which means "stamped" or "impressed" in
a rupam, a likeness or image of something else. The rupee was
stamped in the image of something else. The word for money
was drawn up, feet first, from its Dravidian root uruppu, which
means "from the body"— the body politic in which flesh is a
kind of currency we can use to pay our way into each others'
dreams: first spun from 75% cotton and 25% linen and then
folded in two and placed in a hot purse scented with cinnamon
gum.

M is for Michael Jackson and Malcolm X

In the epilogue to *The Autobiography of Malcolm X*, Alex Haley recounts meeting a pensive Malcolm at the Kennedy airport, watching newly immigrated children "romping and playing" in their sudden home. "By tomorrow night," Malcolm says to Alex, "they'll know how to say their first English word—*nigger.*"

Before cable television arrived in India, America was a white nation. I imagined New England snows dusting California and Miami's beaches stretched across Appalachia. America was a papier-mâché parody patched together by a cheaply hired prop maker. Geographic accuracy was sacrificed to the interpersonal dramas of Betty and Veronica, and the American banquet was limited to the malted and fried offerings in Pop's Chock'lit Shoppe, where the Riverdale gang solved the real geopolitical problems of how to get Reggie off Moose's back with the help of Archie's fumbling charms. Here, class warfare came with a side of fries. There were rumors of distant family members "settling" in "North Dakota" or "Oklahoma"— names that put themselves together like Lego castles: hard-edged and jutting out with an abrupt L or a particularly pokey K.

Blackness was just a rumor too. Blackness flickered in the background of photographs they sent back from these mysterious locations: here's an uncle waving at us from a glittering Times Square (Los Angeles); here's an aunt waving at us mid-way through the soft-focus neon breakfasts with Aunt Jemima's maple syrup (made from maple leaves); here's a nephew waving at us next to the poster of a red and white Michael Jordan in a quilted bedroom, his rotund brown body snuggled in tie-dye and tucked into tartan flannel sheets. Blackness was a rumor, that is, until Michael Jackson's *Bad* ripped into our consciousness and suddenly, knobby-kneed pre-teens found a way to make stringy curls with coconut oil stolen from their mothers' kitchens and started moonwalking backwards into my Social Studies classrooms, all snappy crotch and jaunty limbs. We girls rolled our eyes but we kept on watching.

It wasn't long before Jackson's unsparing gaze, draped in slick black leather, began replacing the glowing pastel Ganeshes and Saraswatis hanging above study desks. But replacing an elephantine god's soft paunch with lean, mean celebrity did not save us from our own ignorance of how blackness and brownness were connected through a struggle for economic self-realization and human rights. While kids in Chennai were rehearsing Michael Peters' signature choreography for "Thriller" and pretending to be zombies— little exemplary half-dead spectacles— Union Carbide was industriously shirking responsibility for the Bhopal Tragedy, which choked thousands of Indians to death, and black mortality was spiking in violent, homicidal protest of the US DEA's drug buys and cocaine busts.

In other words, Tamilians blinked away Michael Jackson's blackness. We kept the heat and thunder of his fat synth bass, which found its way into Ilayaraaja's electric disco in films of the late 1980s like *Vetri Vizha* and *Agni Natchathiram*. We kept the ebullient automation of his moves, which became a muscular theme in Prabhu Deva's blend of baggy breakdance and whimsical terukoothu folk dancing in the 1990s. But we forgot his blackness. In time, the lightning of his presence was replaced by the grey hum of CNN, *Cops, Law & Order*, and the dull horror of handcuffs on dark wrists. Posters yellowed, cassettes spooled out, and my moonwalking classmates found their scientific calculators and study guides again.

But the rumors of racial difference in George Bush Sr.'s America continued to bloom and wilt in morose cycles in my childhood homes into the 1990s. In damp clusters, it grew like moss under rocks. Rootless, it stretched its stringy arms and held us by the ankles; it grew like mold between bathroom tiles; it spun itself fine and strong, webbing into corners where our brooms couldn't reach. In time, the mossy rocks lined our after-dinner walks past the hibiscus bushes. In time, a grandmother slipped on the bathroom tiles and stayed in bed, fed conjee by a fatherless girl brought in from the village and the moss grew between her toes and drew her into the earth where they buried the nameless pets and tossed the chicken feathers. In time, the spiders hung so low they fell into pickle jars every time a child fished for a gooseberry or a slice of stony green mango from the brine. And from this brine, in time, we learned to believe that it existed. And as Tamilian families began drifting from the flashy monsoons of India to the June gloom of the California bay or to the sharp wet summers of the Keys, they carried the damp and stench in suitcases and buried it in hushed conversations. They made a poultice of moss and spider web and lodged it in the prayer books, hung it around the children's necks like a talisman, and they said— *as long as she doesn't marry a black man.*

N is for (The Making of) New Americans

White sateen bodice. Sequined shrug. Ruffled beige bellbottoms.
Cream leather vest over a silver chiffon blouson. Feather-edged
angel cape. A soft shag. A tight curl. Penciled brows. Pointed
lapels. This was the soft-focus dreamlife brought to us by
Agnetha, Björn, Benny, and Anni-Frid. ABBA spun gold from
flax from heartbreak: the genius of pairing a Napoleon jacket
with snake-skin thigh-high boots; of pairing silver epaulettes
with heart-shaped medallions. Military-Disco-Love-Songs.

In 1975, when ABBA's superhit "Fernando" squirrels its way
into the mulled-wine scented plum-cake roofed Anglo-Indian
households of Royapuram, Prime Minister Indira Gandhi has
declared a state of emergency— personal rights are suspended,
properties annexed, the press is censored, thousands of
dissenting civilians and politicians are jailed, a mass-sterilization
campaign is introduced to control a nation jolted into Gandhi's
rule by decree.

But, also in 1975, my father at 19— tapping his feet in
Royapuram's skinny alleys bordered by narrow gutters, in his
skinnier bellbottomed pipes, the massive belt buckle pressing
through his polyester shirt, carrying a Triple-E textbook
bought secondhand on scholarship— is eavesdropping into
ABBA's dreams spinning on a borrowed LP and wafting from
a neighbor's window, while his mother folded one rupee into a
week's dinners like an origami artist and his father bicycled back
from his post at the post office in a pair of frayed grey pants
patched so they made it till Christmas. And all the cardboard

stars swung from electric lines in the alleys. "They were shining there for you and me, for liberty, Fernando."

And that same year, the United States allowed 15,000 Indians to migrate as guest workers.

In San Francisco, forty years later, my father cracks open a bottle of 20-year-old scotch and "Fernando" comes on and my mother and I can hear him tapping his feet in a backyard farther away from an alley in Madras than the cardboard stars of Royapuram's sky were from the Milky Way, keeping time with a dream he lives but can't return to. And I understand, finally, that for him and the millions of men who left kith behind in pursuit of a dream, America is just like ABBA put it: "And how could I ever refuse? I feel like I win when I lose."

O is for Oh

Oh, I love your accent!
Oh, your English is so good, where did you get it!
Oh, can I touch your hair!
Oh, where do you keep all your spices!
Oh, you're lucky you have a year-round tan!
Oh, can we come to your Bollywood wedding!
Oh, so colorful!
Oh, I love culture!
Oh, you're so lucky to have traditions!
Oh, I just have to say it no offence but like!
Oh, I adore curry but I just can't eat it but you should go
　　ahead though!
Oh, when can we come to your arranged marriage!
Oh, will your child be white or Hindu! Technically!
Oh, are you from here-here or like!
Oh, is that like a language or like a religion or whatever!
Oh, are your words upside down and do your people read
　　backwards like the Iraqis!
Oh, where's your Dad's turban!
Oh, I love your food!
Oh, your name is so beautiful and mine is so bleh!
Oh, say can you see!
Oh, say can't you see!

P is for Perfume

Fa is an international brand of deodorants owned by the German company Henkel, which specializes (somewhat unintuitively) in laundry products and adhesives. Fa is also the icon of bathroom shelves (Economy class), dressing tables (Premium Economy class), and dressing rooms (Business class), which has helped my kithwomen smell like Mystic Moments, Romance Moments, and Fantasy Moments— presumably to accommodate the obvious lack of these *moments* in the very boudoirs and bathrooms where they were hosted. Those cool aluminum canisters flush with images of field roses and azure oceans were an early sortie against the feminine palettes of kithhood. They ousted and outmarketed the redolence of our smoky concrete kitchens; the metallic stain of rainwater and rust left on hands holding sewing scissors; the woodsy hasp of dried marikolunthu and silk that wrapped my aunts and grandmothers. The warmth of plumeria and the bright kiss of mint.

Fa also became, thus, the scent of my kithwomen. Every moist, salty, it's-94°-outside hug or chaste, papery cheek-kiss from great grandmothers and not-so-great grand aunts smelled like hotel air freshener and improbable locations for steamy Mills & Boon romances. The Press' imprint— a flourish of pink ampersand ending with a blooming rose— resting above a set of perky whitegirl tits nestled in an angora turtleneck was as misplaced as the promises of Fa. Do Re Me So *Fa.*

Fa was our slim disaster. Downy kithchildren were left stunned and drunk on Fa during Christmas parties. Caterpillar mustaches on Boyz-II-Men cousins shriveled up in honor of Fa's haunting scent— distinctly more poltergeist than elegiac trace. Entire Easter masses turned instantly flammable thanks to Fa's proprietary blend of aerosol and aluminum zirconium; entire households were deodorized out of incense and turmeric, jasmine and frankincense.

Between the 1980s and the 1990s my kithwomen outsourced their bodies to be re-fragranced, sanitized, and olfactorily anesthetized. And their husbands left to Germany, the UAE, and the USA to afford the very aluminum canisters that would make their wives smell like the glossy flaps in fashion magazines, and tickets for the bigger aluminum canisters they flew in while reading them.

R is for Romance or Rate of Return

Pinky D'Souza is the new Music Miss at the Saint So-and-So's
Anglo-Indian Boys School in Chennai. She carries in her purse
a slick plastic make-up compact etched with five serif-heeled
letters: *Lakmé*. Inside her sateen-lined life, the flat make-up
case clacks next to the retractable baton and the clickable red
ballpoints. In front of her desk the boys are lined up on wooden
benches like notes on staves— some with feet hooked under
the seat, little crotchets in pleather Oxfords; some paunchy with
lunch and sleepy slumped arms, full-cream half-nap breves
drowsing to the pianoforte (playing on a cassette uncoiling in an
old Aiwa Two-In-One bought in "The Gulf"); some with arms
wound around the desk quietly digging for an old piece of gum or
long-retired booger nub, sullen F-clefs curved deep into the grain
of their desks falling slowly into the milky languor of a sunboiled
afternoon.

Pinky D'Souza slowly draws out the compact from the silky gleam
of her purse and the compact claps open— and the boys' eyes
with it, round and bright, they are flashing like the mirror in the
case, which is now open to her face like a coy oyster. It catches
the light from the window and glisters Lakmé to boys who are
now open mouthed, watching Miss Pinky D'Souza watch her own
reflection in the glow of ovals— a brown eye and a polished beam
of a nose, a powdery cheek and a dewy philtrum gather in ripples
until their teacher's face slowly pools in front of them. They
watch her daub the fuchsia paste with a bunny puff and lightly
slap her own cheeks into two popped apples as bright and as pink
as the soft mouths gaping awake in khakis and scrunched socks
cuffing stiff, dark legs.

The whirring fan rubs out the sound of traffic; a spit bubble pops. Outside the classroom, Lakshmi, who the boys call Blackie Lakki, the school's janitor, sweeps the corridor in short, hissing strokes. She is hunched over her palm-spine broom and beads of sweat pool in the small of her back. It is absolutely quiet in Music class, and the education is complete.

Lakmé, the Unilever cosmetics brand that bought shares in the imagination of kithwomen, is named after Léo Delibes' 1833 opera set in "the Orient," whose tragic protagonist is named after the goddess of wealth, Lakshmi. In 1989, a century after the opera opened in Paris, when these boys become businessmen, British Airways will borrow the opera's sweeping, sweltering "Flower Duet" and fragrance its flight cabins with the melody of Lakmé's great fear for her father as he travels into the *ville maudite*— the cursed city— "*Je tremble, je tremble d'effroi!*" But as these businessmen pick up their champagne flute and inhale the *chassé* of jet fuel curling into the cabin, Delibes' duet swells to fortissimo and two flower garlands of the "tragic Orient"— one white jasmine, the other rose— coil around their hearts and strangle them away from home. And that rush of blood makes them blush, mistaking as they do trembling for thrill, and *travail* for travel.

S is for Saget, Bob

I fell in love with Bob Saget the same week I decided to trim my eyelashes. If you cut hair it grows back thicker. If you cut your mouth trying to kiss the TV your shame grows back thicker. Bob, you were a whiteness returning home to Honey, your wife. All of America was yours, Bob. In your smart navy blazers and neutral ties you were like a man in a smart navy blazer wearing a neutral tie. You were as opaque as flannel. There was no entering you. I had no option but to eat you whole. You were a Christmas special all year round.

And what do you want, young lady?

A cat because it's soft.

Oh, how about a bath mat, that's soft.

HA HA. Oh, Bob.

And here's another young lady. Turn around so everyone can see how pretty you are! And now what would you like?

A Baby.

I don't think I can help you with that. But we'll see what we can do.

Bob, you're killing me!

Thank you. You may sit down please.

(Divya. Divya, you're kissing the TV again.)

I would watch you. I would watch you at dinner and I would
soak my papadum in the yogurt until they were paler versions of
the soft supple brown things my sharp brown angles could never
imagine: cheerleader buns, dinner buns, doughnut crèmes, the
mound of a turkey tanning in thanks, Michael Jordon's glossy
printed calves in a grown man's bedroom, the slow motion
slump of a hammock soft with a fat so-and-so. And then I would
rip it apart, weeping in curd, and watch how easily things broke
on screen: kayaks into caravans, kids into cots, yards of crisp
wrapping paper shredded by tall six-year-olds in socks, blondes
named Kevin or Kyle— small boy-birds running screaming from
slushy dogs, a drain pipe weighed by a Wyoming winter claiming
a puff-ball beanie. And then I would eat you. I would eat you
and wash you down with the grainy timestamps on the VHS
tapes they all sent for your love. Bob, I thought you made these
things happen— the brightest front rows of enameled teeth on
the wide-mouths in the front row, this laughter— this, and the
short queue of sleepy hatted black dominoes crashing down on
the church pew. The red, white, and blue, oh the funniest thing
you do, America, America, I want you.

T is for Tamil Filems & Thunderthighs

It is not difficult to find love in Tamil Cinema— it is pulped
and milked and doused in this substance. Its symptoms are
specific— sharing one Thums Up cola (and, for the particularly
scandalous, with one straw); kissing a flower while pouting at
your lover; feeding butter-creamed birthday cake to your lover's
mouth; accidentally ripping your lover's shirt while patting her
on the shoulder; slapping your lover until she realizes she's your
lover; strangling your lover until she succumbs to your good
intentions— but the sentiment is universal: kithwomen love *love*
but they need to be shown that they do.

From Tamil cinema we learned how to drop our eyes when
strangers' gazes glazed up and down our still skinned shins and
to bite our lips when auto-rickshaw drivers and bus conductors
licked theirs at us; how to pull up the sock, pull down the hem,
pull up the neckline, pull down the lids; pull up the dupatta;
pull back, pull back, withdraw, withdraw, hold fire; how to walk
backwards and out of a living room, modestly, with an empty
coffee tray and a full bosom; how to twist free a wrist grabbed
by a greasy boss while also batting our lashes; how to stand for
long periods in the rain in transparent saris weaving around tired,
collapsing bodies in the studio— 1-2, 3, 4, 2-2, 3, 4. We learned
these lessons with every vamp number (1960s), every record
dance (1970s), every dream sequence (1980s), and every item
number (1990s) that sold me on love as it sold me to it.

Silk Smitha and others like her, made of chiffon and Vaseline,
slicked their way across their own brief filmi histories as

contortionists on our celluloid pyres. They sweated through our screens as disembodied navels floating in a storm; as cleaving sets of breasts in steamy kitchens; as body shields for the children being dragged out to the street; as hooks or racks on which belts and bottles are tossed; as bulletproof vests for surly girlchildren speaking out of turn; as supine, crumpled things at the feet of something made of stone, or gold, or bone— husbands, johns, gurus, Shivas, Rams, and so on and so on.

And yet, there is what is left of them— Silk Smitha and her tribe— in my longing to see familiar bodies as I leave a cabaret at Roxy's in Buffalo, snow-collared and highbuttoned. What they gave back to kithwomen— their thunderthighs and lovehandles, their full clavicles and soft jawlines, their dusky armpits and salty stares before kith began paying for whitened and straightened imports dubbing their way into crotches and wallets— is a kind of company we keep in cold weather as we try Spinning® our way to the unimaginable legs that walk the miles imagined by others for our journeys.

U is for Unchristen

Eleven days later pulled from the womb laid on a straw map on a
warm lap a black string with a token of gold tied around a waist
soft with mother's milk and a black khol dot placed on a cheek
to smudge a perfect form to cast away the evileyes of onlookers
someone whispers a name four times into your ear and from the
wilderness you walk in you come in she comes into the home by
a name you call her they call him into being here she is they are
named.

Namakarana or naming ceremony is one of the 16 saṃskāras,
sacraments, undergone by an infant a few days after birth. And
several years from birth, when that infant transcends the womb
and enters the tomb of human resources, they are re-baptized in
their host countries— syllables yanked and consonants snipped
until their names mangle themselves into an American name tag
or a greeting in a call center, balled up to fit like a hardboiled
sweet on the American tongues of those who now call them call
them call them— "Hello, I'm Chris (I used to be Krishnamurthy
Sundararajan). How may I help you?"

Abe, I unchristen you Abhimanyu
Bob, I unchristen you Balakanthan
Chris, I unchristen you Krishnamurthy
Dan, I unchristen you Dhanabaalan
Ellie, I unchristen you Eaellisaichelvi
Gerry, I unchristen you Giribaalan
Harry, I unchristen you Hariharan
Jess, I unchristen you Jeyashanthi

Kat, I unchristen you Kathirselvan
Lucky, I unchristen you Lakshmidevi
Manny, I unchristen you Manoharan
Nat, I unchristen you Nataraajan
Ollie, I unchristen you Oliveanthan
PJ, I unchristen you Poongulazhi
Reggie, I unchristen you Raguvaran
Sandy, I unchristen you Sindhamani
Tammy, I unchristen you Tamizhselvi
Vinny, I unchristen you Vinothan

and finally,

YoLo, I unchristen you Yogya-Loganathan, because, you
know, YOLO.

V is for Vande Mataram

In some living rooms in India (1990)

Father: "'The Last Waltz'— O yes, thizsong— Chyle, lizzen— this one, vee love it— vee used to lizzen, no, during my college days an' ell. This chap Englebert Humperdinck was 'is name— Indian feller 'ee is— Madras feller, yes 'ee was Anglo then itself— those days all those fellers were— "

Child: "Da, why is he named after a 19th-century German composer, then? Ma, whas this man's real Indian name?"

Mother: "Arnold George Dorsey— "

Father: " 'is father was one Irish guy and 'is mudda vas one German lady I think. But this chap is Indian. 100%."

[Exeunt]

In other living rooms in India (2015)

A group of nearly one hundred Hindu men gathered outside Mohammed Akhlaq's home in Dadri, Uttar Pradesh. Enraged by a rumor that Akhlaq's family had consumed beef, they dragged the forty-year-old father out of his house and beat him to death. They kicked his mother, assaulted his daughter, and attempted to beat his brother to death.

W is for Walt Whitman's Soul

One of the very first Indian words to enter the English
language was the Hindustani slang for plunder: "loot."

WILLIAM DALRYMPLE

It sits with a fork made from a lotus on an ivory chair eating
an elephant steak in the company of bears and feral nautch
girls on a monsoon evening incandescent with an appetite as
mighty as railroads spann'd across seas and reclines, its cheeks
burnished, its ass varnished by suns setting on bronze and
sugared with saltpetre, its torso a tableaux for the annals of
rectitude, the theatre for roiling or robust passage, a veritable
Suez Canal towards missionary victories which thrust from such
bejeweled and oiled loins anointed by coin— that emission
of plump plums, lump sums into the Ganges, that coiling coy
virgin maiden winding her languid locks, batting her lashes to
its lashes— its spine a gentle wire. Supine, its belly swells with
salt and figs with meat and treaties, it corks open a profound
song— *itself it sings* into books heavy with truths on the
chair dressed with leather and raw hides kissed by ox blood
smeared with beef dung lined with raw silk woven from worms
plucked from boughs basted across its pious beaming eyes its
spidery ghosted lids, and its byzantine glance unmoors from its
Chinese porcelain and crosses the ebony table polished with
lac secreted from the cloaca of the *kerria lacca* set with glazed
cakes eaten by pinked mouths wearing crimson robes, to its
guests polished and glossed and stained by the ooze drawn to
color the uncolored raw linen, the wood, the human. Then its
wrist cuffed by gold and cowries and studded with coral draws

a whisper-thin muslin veil dyed carmine— sucked from crushed
scale of cochineal boiled in ammonia and bled into curds and
rouge glinting sanguineous and turbid between bug and rug snug
a thug in redcoat or a turncoat carrying urns of this stuff— from
estates of cocoa coconut calico— across its face while soft éclairs
of chocolate bumble out from its plumed rump choked with gum
and linseed flax and cassia cinnamon and pepper like so many
lines of blood underwriting the mutton and not the goat so it
can it sell them with *a name of a place* like scarves or garlanded
whores moored to wharves suckled by mother of pearl or teas
named after Earls and they with whole scores to settle settle for
homemade cures nettles ginger turmeric— a paste or to taste—
and it steals and seals in letters scented with sandal sent abroad
waxed and pressed with cornelian gems honed from ground it
owns and makes stone from their flesh ekes ink from their sweat
soaks indigo in lye fermented with time and makes color so it can
bid for its own passage, the passage, O of this soul, to India!

Notes

1. Kith & Prologue

Opening tale
I am indebted to Ramki Uncle for the root of this story, which he
shared in El Sobrante, California in the Summer of 2015. Like all
storytellers, I then took a cutting to grow something that is not mine to
keep.

Opening dedication
I borrow language here from Vijay Prashad's *The Karma of Brown Folk*,
where he quotes the American missionary R. S. Minturn reporting on
his travels in Calcutta, India.

2. Dromomanie

This portion of the manuscript draws from tales told to me by family
members over the course of my life— many of them elaborate fictions
and many of them necessarily true. I attribute these particularly to
Helen Simon of Villikuri; Cecily Victor of Nagercoil; Rani Rajasekaran
of Kanyakumari District; the Sanskrit epic, *Rāmāyaṇa* by Valmiki.
I learned also about early Indian traders and merchants from the
exquisite and laborious research of Vivek Bald in *Bengali Harlem and
the Lost Histories of South Asian America*.

3. Paper People

I am indebted here to the imaginaries of bell hooks; Gloria Anzaldua;
the musical phrase of Objectivist aesthetics, as articulated in Charles
Reznikoff's interview with L. S. Dembo; and Maestro Ilayaraaja's score
for Mani Ratnam's *Nayagan*.

4. Paper Boats

"Thenpandi Cheemayile," written by Pulamaipithan, scored by Maestro Ilayaraaja: I am indebted to American poet Rob Halpern (his listening to my Americanized rendition of this song in his home) and fellow Tamilian poet Shivram Gopinath (who celebrated this song in my home in Singapore) whose thinking and feeling along its notes helped me write this section, which was until then a "shriek frightful" waiting to be sung.

5. Water

Water
Portions of this section draw language from the Gospel of Luke and the Gospel of John, concerning the Miraculous Draught of Fishes, a narrative which allegorizes the shift in apostolic labor from harvesting natural resources to biopolitical headhunting.

Interlude
"Water, water" is drawn from Samuel Taylor Coleridge's *The Rime of the Ancient Mariner* (text of 1834).

Pearl & Peril
I draw from multiple news sources, particularly "Human Tooth Found in McDonald's Japan Fries: Fast Food Operator Reports Four Cases of Contaminated Food" by Megumi Fujikawa, *The Wall Street Journal*; "Woman at Franklin Restaurant" by Nick Calloway, News2 WKRN Nashville (*ABC News*).

Marine Snow
I am indebted to the work of Henk-Jan Hoving and Senior Scientist Bruce Robison of the Monterey Bay Aquarium on the feeding habits of Vampyroteuthis infernalis.

Interlude
"this is how an ocean is told." For this sentiment I am indebted to
those living in the locale of Kanyakumari District, Tamil Nadu, who
made their living from fishing until industrialized fishing staggered
genealogy and trade in the 1960s.

6. Blood

i. No English. Indian. Walking.

I am deeply indebted to the passionate and incisive research of Vijay
Prashad in his book *The Karma of Brown Folk*, and the compassionate
informal journalism of Maria Giovanna in her memorial for Navroze
Modi on her blog *Filmiholic* (31 March 2008). I also draw from Henry
Gray's description of angiology in *Anatomy of the Human Body* and
Cennino Cennini's *The Craftsman's Handbook: The Italian "Il Libro
dell'Arte"*, translated by Daniel V. Thompson, Jr.

ii. A Sequence of Unbearable Happenings

I draw on the collective labor of the book and website *Without
Sanctuary: Photographs and Postcards of Lynchings in America*.

iii. An Unknown Length of Rope

I learned from the research of art historians and curators: J. V. S.
Megaw, "Something Old, Something New: Further Notes on the
Aborigines of the Sydney District as Represented by their Surviving
Artefacts, and as Depicted in Some Early European Representations"
(Records of the Australian Museum Supplement, 1993); E. P.
Richardson's notes on John Singleton Copley's *Head of a Negro* in the
Bulletin of the Detroit Institute of Arts (Number 3, 1952-1953); the
staff writers for the National Gallery of Art, Washington, D. C.; David

Bjelajac, *American Art: A Cultural History*; Marcus Rediker, *The Slave Ship: A Human History*.

I am also particularly indebted to Robert Hayden's poem *Middle Passage* and to Douglas Kearney's oeuvre, which helps me work through the fissure between the spectacle and the spectacular.

iv. A Laundry List

I learned through and borrowed language from Flora Annie Steel and Grace Gardiner's *The Complete Indian Housekeeper and Cook*, written as a primer for "the English girls to whom fate may assign the task of being house-mothers in our eastern empire."

7. Salt

I owe my awareness of this event to the compassionate coverage of the plight of salt flat laborers by Suzanne Goldenberg, "Storm haunts the forgotten labourers of the salt-pans," *The Guardian* (11 February 1999); by a staff writer for *The Hindu*, "Salt pan workers of the Rann of Kutch" (13 January 2013); by Rupam Jain Nair, "Salt mining leaves bitter taste for Indian workers," *The Telegraph* (24 February 2010).

10. Foreign Terms

For this section, I owe:

Mary Leech, "Big Sur Field Guide/Guide to the Geology of the
        California Coast." San Francisco State University (2006)
Walter Benn Michaels, *The Trouble with Diversity: How We Learned to
    Love Identity and Ignore Inequality*.

Phrase Book: Or, Idiomatic Expressions in English and Tamil. Designed
to assist Tamil Youths in the Study of the English Language.
C. Rajagopalachari, *Mahabharata.*
Rainer Maria Rilke, "Portrait of My Father as a Young Man," translated
    by Stephen Mitchell.
Walt Whitman, *Leaves of Grass.*

The immigrant's dance is always a ricochet of limbs. As Amitava
Kumar acknowledges, "What I am always going back to is the moment
when I was going away." For my thinking in this section I owe much
to what I've learned from his quenching, lucid writing— a sense of
the importance of objects, of the emotional reserve of import-export,
of nostalgia as a kind of political salvage. He captures this particularly
well in an essay in *Bombay—London—New York*: "I am not distrustful
of my nostalgia—I think nostalgia can be a weapon in a cultural
milieu where you are expected to feel only shame for what you have
left behind—but I do want to ask what it means to remember. Clearly,
there is more than merely the calculus of loss in what one can call,
borrowing a phrase from Salman Rushdie, the business of 'nostalgia
economics.'" Indeed. And I wanted to ask, borrowing a phrase from
Arundhati Roy, how "the checkbook and the cruise missile" were part
of the affective economy of my grandmother's custards.

e

Acknowledgements for photographs.

All photographs in the book have been sourced from my family's albums. Wherever possible, I've tried to reach out to those whose photographs have been included—Helen and A.R. Simon; Cecily and John Victor Pudota; Merlin; Felix, Isabel, Kishore Fernands; Drs. Rachel Reddy, Teresa Simon, Alex Simon, Beena Stanley— and thank the many whose names or contacts have been sealed in old address books, letters, and the memories of my grandparents, to which I have no access.

Acknowledgements and thanks.

My thanks to the editors who helped versions of texts from *Kith* appear before they were gathered here: Anselm Berrigan for *The Brooklyn Rail*, Desmond Kon for *Kitaab: Asia+n Writing in English*, Soham Patel for *Cream City Review*, Michael Nardone for *The Elephants* and *HOBO*, Dawn Lundy Martin for *boundary2*, Douglas Kearney for *BAX: Best American Experimental Writing*, Isabel and Rita Campos for *Sputnik and Fizzle*, David Buuck for *Tripwire*, NatalieAnn Rich for *A Women's Thing*.

My thanks to the curators and organizers of readings and festivals who helped these texts gain voice and body, over the last many years: Pooja Nansi (Speakeasy), Desmond Kon and Yeow Kai Chai (Singapore Writers' Festival), Samantha Giles (The Leslie Scalapino Memorial Lecture in 21st Century Poetics/Small Press Traffic), Robin Hemley and Heidi Stalla (Yale-NUS), Darryl Whetter (LASALLE), Stephanie Chan Dogfoot (SPEAK), Joseph Mosconi and Andrew Maxwell (Poetic Research Bureau), Teresa Carmody (Les Figues), Alli Warren (The Wattis Institute), Caleb Beckwith and Turner Canty (Sponge), Mat Laporte and Eric Schmaltz (Contemporary Poetry Research Group).

ſ

My thanks to the artists Karin Aue, Joseph Mosconi, Sophia Le Fraga, and Fia Backström, who took *Kith* and made it manifest through their voice, illustrations, bodies, and installation.

The research and travel undertaken for *Kith* has been supported by funding from Nanyang Technological University.

This book would just be a file in my hard drive were it not for the vision and optimism of Rebecca Wolff and Jay and Hazel MillAr, who saw *Kith* as a book even before I could, and believed in this project with great patience as I continued working on it. I am grateful to my elders Dee Morris, Myung Mi Kim, Rachel Blau DuPlessis, and Vanessa Place who supported me as poets, scholars, feminists, and mothers while I edited this book, wrung myself on the academic market, carried my first child, and planned yet another migration across the Atlantic.

Amitava Kumar, Douglas Kearney, and Rachel Zolf: your sensibility, ethos, and genius keeps me grounded and inspired and your work shows me what is at stake in every utterance, every edit— I am grateful for your help in presenting this work's face to the world. Thank you, Barrie Sherwood, Kevin Riordan, and Jen Crawford— my colleagues at Nanyang Technological University— you supported my rookie years and lent clarity, practical judgment, and humor through my time in Singapore. For her careful eye as my Tamil editor, my thanks to Usha Rajan. *Kith's* voice is, in part, sourced from my own evolution as a teacher of poetics, and for this I am indebted to my students Arin Fong, Diyana Sastrawati Mohamad, Isabelle Teo, James Kuwik, Marylyn Tan, Megan Weal, Nurul Wahidah binte Mohd. Tambee, Patricia Karunungan, Reginald James Kent, Samuel Caleb Wee, Victoria Iacchetta and all the adventurous writers at the University at Buffalo and NTU— thank you for carrying my voice to your ears and helping me understand what I was saying. I hope you write your endless, beautiful selves always.

g

My dad and mum, Victor and Ammani, and paati, Helen, who laughed, sighed, and wept through what I shared from this project: you are the book's true archive and without you it simply would not exist. *Kith* exists first for this kin. And it exists too for my kith in Singapore and the United States, who made sure this project remained buoyant, possible, and necessary in my own life— I am so grateful for the conversations I've had with all of you around this book— CA Conrad, Caleb Beckwith, Karin Aue, Sarah Dowling, Shiv Kotecha, Mrigaa Sethi, Shivram Gopinath, Alli Warren, Gordon Faylor, Hugo García Manríquez, and Rob Halpern. And finally, Josh Lam— *Kith* exists because you are my first reader, my truest witness and a selfless editor: *kora kaagaz tha ye mann mera/ likh liya naam is pe tera.*